LIMIT LESS

Radhika
Gupta

LIMITLESS

The
Power of
Unlocking
Your True
Potential

hachette
INDIA

First published in 2022 by Hachette India
(Registered name: Hachette Book Publishing India Pvt. Ltd)
An Hachette UK company
www.hachetteindia.com

1

ISBN 978-93-91028-50-3

Hachette Book Publishing India Pvt. Ltd
4th & 5th Floors, Corporate Centre,
Plot No. 94, Sector 44, Gurugram 122003, India

Typeset in Sabon LT Std 11.5/17
by R. Ajith Kumar, New Delhi

Printed and bound in India
by Manipal Technologies Limited, Manipal

MIX
Paper from
responsible sources
FSC™ C043100

CONTENTS

INTRODUCTION

VINITA IS A STUDENT AT AN ENGINEERING COLLEGE IN Pune. In her family, she is not only the first girl to have left her home city to study outside but is also the first prospective engineer. Every girl, she says, should make 'use of every opportunity she has and every resource she is provided'. Vinita is driven, ambitious, and clearly wants to be someone. And yet she feels more than a little low – this is the last week of her final year at engineering college, and she has been rejected by five companies during the campus placement process.

Prateek is 32 years old. He graduated from business school nine years ago and works for a well-known multi-national company in Mumbai. His work hours are comfortable and he has been with the company for five years. He is paid well enough and has received two promotions since he joined. In his own words, though, he is bored out of his mind. 'My job,' he writes, 'is drudgery, and it is pretty obvious I am not going anywhere, even though it seems I have everything.' He wants to try something different – joining in a higher position in a smaller company, starting his own business, just anything that is different really. He wants to take a risk. But he just can't seem to make that jump.

Sonali works for an information technology company in Bengaluru in the human resources (HR) department and wants to go to the United States (US) for her master's degree. She describes herself as someone who wishes to step out of her comfort zone and constantly pushes herself to be her best. Sonali has had a bald patch on her head since the age of 11. It bothered her as a teenager and it bothers her now. Sometimes, in a new environment, she fears that people 'will notice only her scanty hair and it will ruin first impressions'.

These are three real stories (names have been changed to protect individual privacy) from the many that sit in my inbox daily. The people who write these mails are unknown to me, but their stories are strikingly familiar.

I have grappled with many of the same questions

in my life and lived some of these stories. In 2005, after being rejected by seven consulting firms back-to-back during campus placements at the University of Pennsylvania (UPenn), I tried to jump off the nineteenth floor of a building. I was a 21-year-old college student then and I didn't know how to handle being told 'no'. Thankfully, my then classmate and now husband, Nalin, came to my rescue (something he still does in many situations) and, as it happens with most of us, my life turned out fairly fine. I ended up starting my career at McKinsey, and then cut my teeth as an analyst on Wall Street in the mid-2000s at a boutique hedge fund called AQR Capital Management (AQR). In 2009, I moved back to India to start my own asset management company (AMC) with two of my UPenn classmates. We named it Forefront Capital Management (Forefront) and later sold it to a larger Indian financial services firm, Edelweiss Financial Services.

Today, as the MD and CEO of Edelweiss Mutual Fund (Edelweiss MF), I sell mutual funds for a living, and on most days I wake up thinking I have one of the best jobs on earth. In 2018, 13 years after the incident at UPenn, I decided to tell my story in a video titled 'The Girl with a Broken Neck'. To this day, I am surprised by the number of people across generations and different walks of life who have connected with my story, in whole or in part.

Stories are powerful creatures. When I chose to share mine, I was suddenly flooded with mails like the ones I've mentioned. These mails have an interesting duality to them. On the one hand, they are inspirational stories of men and women with high aspirations who want the best for themselves – young Indians who want to rise above their circumstances and excel. On the other, they speak volumes about the limitations that hold each of us back – both the internal ones, imposed by our own minds, a function of our backgrounds, and the external ones that are gradually increasing in an Instagram-fed, comparison-fuelled world.

Initially, I used to wonder why people shared these incredibly poignant stories with me or addressed complex questions to someone unknown to them. I have now come to realize that stories aren't easily shared and guidance isn't easy to come by. Difficult discussions about rejection, risk, imperfection and self-confidence aren't exactly dinner table conversations in Indian homes. Most of us are building careers in industries that are vastly different from those that existed in our parents' generation. The times they lived in were very different too. Our challenges are not the ones they faced. Often, we don't have a ready-made professional network to guide us, especially in the early and formative years of our careers, and even when we do we find it hard to ask for help.

The mails I receive ask important questions: What do we do if life hands us a career we don't love? How do we seek help and guidance at work when we are stuck but too shy to ask for help? How do we find the courage to have open conversations that can make our daily lives smoother and less stressful? This book is my attempt to tackle these questions – the ones I have asked myself and perhaps the ones some of you have faced – and the answers I would have written to my 21-year-old self.

I sometimes wonder if I was meant to write this book. My writing has so far been limited to short posts on social media, and I never imagined that a busy career and a full life would allow me the time to write an entire book. It was always my post-retirement plan. Yet, a chance conversation and life in lockdown during the COVID-19 pandemic changed all that.

This book is not an autobiography or a memoir. It does, however, draw on life stories – both my own and of those who have taught me something. My learnings are not necessarily new, and I can't pretend to have conquered all the issues I've addressed in the book. In fact, I occasionally continue to struggle with them. But I hope that my stories will connect with you and encourage you to share your own, because every story shared has the power to exponentially influence others.

I also hope this book will start some much-needed conversations. Our news and media are full of stories highlighting starting salaries at campuses, but I would love to see an India that also talks about how to handle failure. Every unicorn is an achievement and should be celebrated, but I would love to hear discussions about the things that hold a young person back from taking even small risks, like changing jobs when they are unhappy. There is nothing wrong with the lists that rank the 'most powerful people' and 'the richest people', but what about a dialogue on the bad days, the dark days, the vulnerable sides of both the cubicle and corner office? Who's answering them?

For every person encouraging me to write this book, there was also someone telling me that I am too young to write it – and for the longest time I too believed the latter. But perhaps this was one more limitation that I arbitrarily placed on myself. This book reflects my voice today, a voice that I know will evolve with time and age. Ten years later, perhaps a different me will reject some of what I have said here. We grow, we learn and we change!

I am in the capital markets business, and I am fundamentally bullish on India. We live in an era defined by growth and opportunities. India is buzzing, and how! When I moved back to the country from the US in 2009, I was asked a lot of questions about whether I thought I was doing the right thing. I feel there has never been a better time to be a young Indian. Career options are wider than they ever have been before, and you can make a mark in any space you set out to – from food to financial services. You can start life from a small town near Nagpur and list your company on the National Stock Exchange a decade later. Yet, even as our markets hit all-time highs, we live in a time in which mental health challenges, at home and at work, are also rampant. And while webinars and connectivity have zoomed forward in a world grappling with COVID-19, the meaningful conversations we have are much fewer.

Speaking of conversations, a question I get asked by young people very often is what I do to get big returns from the markets. For this, I have one answer. Yes, my business is called asset management and it is money that is referred to as an asset. But I truly believe that, as individuals, our biggest asset is our inherent talent. Each one of us needs to maximize the potential of this asset to live as a version of ourselves that is free of self-doubt and limitations. Serious and mindful investment in your talent and abilities will create more wealth for you in the long run than any stock, bond or financial instrument.

How do you earn the highest rate of return on yourself, you ask? Read on.

KICKING THE S**T OUT OF REJECTION

REJECTION: KNOW THAT IT'S A PART OF THE SYLLABUS

'I love my rejection slips. They show me I try.'

– Sylvia Plath

AFTER GRADUATING FROM COLLEGE, AMITABH Bachchan, who was struggling to find a job, applied to All India Radio (AIR), hoping to land an opportunity as a newsreader or commentator. The man and his now legendary baritone voice were rejected, for both English and Hindi broadcasts. He went on to deliver 12 flop movies before *Zanjeer* became a blockbuster.

After Vidya Balan was roped in as the female lead for a Malayalam film, *Chakram*, opposite a prominent superstar, she was signed on for 12 more films in the industry. However, *Chakram* was shelved due to production snags. The shelving of a film starring such a major star was at the time unheard of in the industry, and in interviews she recalls producers blaming her for being the jinx and replacing her in all the other Malayalam films as well.

Film buffs like me hoard facts like these. Yet, despite knowing that some of the most successful people in Indian cinema have had epic trysts with failure, why did getting rejected seven times by recruiters while I was at UPenn feel like the end of the world to me? Why did I handle my first encounter with rejection so badly? Was it because it was seven rejections in a row? Perhaps. Was it because I desperately wanted that job at that seventh company, a well-known finance-focused consulting firm? Not really. I did want a consulting job, but I had no particular affection for the firm in question. It could have been any other firm and I would have felt the same way.

If I had to be brutally honest, I would have to admit that I felt my disappointment so acutely because while they had rejected me they offered jobs to three friends in our Indian circle at the university. In my mind, I was better, at least academically. Yet, my friends had the consulting jobs and I didn't. Radhika Gupta – a member of the most prestigious joint-degree programme on campus, the topper who helped everyone else with their homework, the student who had cracked a top-notch internship at Microsoft in her second year – had failed. She had failed spectacularly and publicly, in her final year, when the stakes were the highest.

There is a scene in the movie *3 Idiots* in which Raju and Farhan – played by Sharman Joshi and R. Madhavan respectively – realize that they have come last and second to last in their final exams. They feel relieved that they have passed, but then they worry that their friend Rancho (played by Aamir Khan) may have failed. When they realize that, far from failing, Rancho has come first, their sense of relief about their situation quickly turns to misery. They tell each other, '*Dost* fail *ho jaaye toh dukh hota hai, lekin dost* first *aaye toh aur dukh hota hai.*' When a friend fails you feel bad, but when a friend comes first you feel worse.

Campus placements were my first real experience of rejection, and I was totally unprepared to deal with it. Most of us are. We grow up hearing, '*Beta,* work hard. Keep studying. Be focused.' If we do these things, we are told, we will get into a good school, and

HANDLING FAILURE IS AN IMPORTANT LESSON TO MASTER, BECAUSE EVEN THE HARD WORK VARIABLE ONLY GOES SO FAR.

then a good college, and thereafter a good job is assured. But what if we follow the script and work hard and, despite giving it our very best shot, fail? Which syllabus has the formula to deal with that? To whom do we turn to understand what has happened, and what do we do to cope? Handling failure is an important lesson to master, because even the hard work variable only goes so far. As we grow up, success evolves into a complex multi-variable equation. How we communicate, the confidence we project, our ability to network, how we fare in critical moments relative to others – all of this begins to play a part in the outcome and most of us end up struggling. In India, where lakhs of people apply for everything, from the civil services examinations to a shot at *Indian Idol*, it is a question of *when* we will experience failure, not *if* we will. At some point, each of us will face rejection of some kind. That is a guarantee.

The biggest mistake I made when I was rejected by the seventh company was to not give myself time to let the rejection sink in, absorb it and share what I felt about it. Rejection hurts; it is humiliating. When it is continuous, it crushes your self-esteem and throws you into a vicious cycle of self-doubt. A voice in your head keeps asking you, 'Am I capable of anything at all?' At the same time, people around us either tell us that things will get better or push us to be strong. As many of you will know, at that point, strength is the last thing on your mind and it feels like things will never get better.

Devanshi Jalan, a psychologist and a friend, once told me that when you are deeply upset it's important to just sit with that feeling, to 'feel it to heal it', and I think she is absolutely right. In my case, while dealing with the multiple rejections, I cut myself off from the world for fear of being judged and didn't speak to anybody about it except Nalin. It's not that I didn't have friends or a support system, but I just didn't speak out. Fifteen years later, after I told this story in public, my roommate in college and a very close friend today wrote me a message saying, 'Babe, I am sorry I didn't know what you were going through. I wish I was there.' I told her it wasn't her fault. How would she have known if I didn't tell her about it?

I wasn't the only one going through this. At UPenn, most third year students (juniors, in American parlance) took on internships at large banks and technology firms and, at the end of the summer, received returning offers (pre-placement offers, in Indian parlance) to join after graduation.

Having a returning offer gave you a leg up as you entered placement season in your fourth year. While 80–90 per cent of students got returning offers, there were many who didn't, and this was not always because of poor work performance. Not only did such students usually have it much harder in the placement season – few companies wanted to hire someone who was 'rejected' by their last employer – they also lost face in front of classmates. They went from being the student who had the glory of interning at Goldman Sachs to being labelled a 'reject' at their first job. I know many people who went through this – smart, hardworking professionals, who may have had a rough boss or a genuine issue fitting into an organization – and while they were going through hell, they never spoke about it, even with their closest friends. Very few people had the courage to ask for help, or proactively reach out to someone willing to lend a hand. What started with returning offers on campus repeats even today when people lose their jobs – often, again, for no fault of their own. It is a battle that many of us fight privately and silently.

Hearing 'no' is never easy, but it is not as personal as we think it is. I've heard it a lot over the years.

A few years after joining my first job at McKinsey (that story comes later!), I joined the asset management business, where selling financial products to

AT SOME POINT, EACH OF US WILL FACE REJECTION OF SOME KIND. THAT IS A GUARANTEE.

potential distributors and clients is an important part of the job. In sales, 'no' is a word you hear every day. You may have the best product, but the chances that a customer or distributor will refuse to hand you money in exchange for it are reasonably high, especially if you don't represent an established brand. I didn't do a lot of sales in my first asset management role at AQR but Forefront was a start-up and sales was a big part of what I had to do. Nine out of every 10 attempts I made to convert a lead ended up failing, and when customers and distributors told me they didn't want to work with us I used to get upset and agitated. I was convinced that their 'no' was a personal attack on me and the Forefront brand. As far as I was concerned, they didn't want to work with us because they didn't take us seriously enough on account of being a young company.

Years later, however, the same people who said 'no' to us at first became some of our most loyal customers and partners. What changed? In some cases, initially, our products didn't suit their needs, but later we had something that did. In some cases, they wanted to see a certain commitment to and maturity in the business, which only came with time. And, in 99 per cent of the cases, the rejection was about our product, our track record or a better alternative being available, not about us at a personal level. If the rejection was personal, it would have been permanent.

Most often, it is an idea that is rejected, not an individual. I couldn't appreciate this during my UPenn and Forefront days, but today, as someone who sits on the other side of the table to hire candidates, I know that for each position we hope to fill there are usually three or four people we would be more than happy to hire. The choice of A over B is not a reflection of B's shortcomings, but usually just the fact that A is a better fit. If we could, we would hire both A and B, and even C!

Speaking of alphabets, all of us have something that we really want to do – let's call that our Option A – and we fall head over heels in love with the idea of it. This is one of the reasons rejection is so tough for us to deal with. If the dream job, the dream partner, or the dream home that we work all our lives for don't come our way, we are shattered. While there is nothing wrong with having an Option A, it is important to remember that in life we always have Option Bs and they aren't usually compromises either. My consulting career was my Option A at UPenn. I forgot – though my parents kept reminding me – that I had a solid Option B: two summer internships at Microsoft and a confirmed pre-placement offer from them before I started the search for a consulting position. Microsoft was a place I enjoyed working at, a place that would pay me well. It was a real option, and a good one at that. In hindsight I know that if the McKinsey opportunity hadn't cropped up, life would have worked out just fine for me at Microsoft.

Over the years, I have learnt not to limit my definition of success to a single option, because I have experienced the power of Option B. Most consultants, after their two-year programme, apply to private equity and venture capital firms as a next step; it's the thing to do and that's what I did after my stint at McKinsey. I got an interview with every big private equity

> **OVER THE YEARS, I HAVE LEARNT NOT TO LIMIT MY DEFINITION OF SUCCESS TO A SINGLE OPTION, BECAUSE I HAVE EXPERIENCED THE POWER OF OPTION B.**

firm, but I didn't get a single offer – not even from smaller outfits that I interviewed at next. At the same time, I received an interview opportunity from AQR, which happened to be founded by Cliff Asness, who had attended the same programme I graduated in at UPenn. AQR was a quantitatively focused company run by academically oriented professionals, and Cliff was the chief nerd there. My finance and computer science backgrounds were a good fit for them. Quantitative investing and AQR were never a part of my post-McKinsey plan, but with Option A gone, this was what I had left. I rose up the ranks to become a fund manager at AQR, which grew quickly in the Wall Street boom of the mid-2000s. Forefront was later built on the same principles of quantitative investing. Was AQR an inferior option to working in private equity? I don't know, but it enabled me to come back to India and start a fund business of my own at the age of 24 and, more than that, it helped me transition into the role that I have today. A very important part of what we do at Edelweiss MF is quantitative and process-driven investing, and my Option B experience at one of the world's leading quantitative funds has come in handy.

Focus is important, but always give yourself a

few degrees of freedom. Do not chase a single door – rather, hope for a few different doors to open, knowing that whichever one you walk into will lead to a meaningful opportunity, if you choose to make it one.

Besides, what is a great saga without stories of failure? Former American President Theodore (Teddy) Roosevelt, spoke passionately about it more than a century ago: 'It is not the critic who counts. The credit belongs to the man in the area, whose face is marred by dust and sweat, who strives, who errs, who comes short again and again, who at the best knows the triumph of achievement, and at the worst, if he fails, fails while daring greatly.'

When ambition is involved, rejection is almost inevitable. At McKinsey, one of my early projects was a high-profile case in a team with a whopping 15 members (usually project teams have four or five people). The group was broken into three workstreams, with a

WHEN AMBITION IS INVOLVED, REJECTION IS ALMOST INEVITABLE.

senior associate (SA, usually an MBA with a few years of experience) leading a few analysts (recent undergraduates) on each team. A senior engagement management (SEM) ran the project and managed day-to-day relationships with the clients while also handling partners of the firm who oversaw the project. One week into the project, the SA started having issues with the SEM, and by the second week it was clear that the latter wasn't happy with the SA either. This led to the SEM distancing the SA from the project (the SA eventually quit), and a lot of work being diverted to me, including handling client teams myself – something analysts don't usually do. It was hard work, but a fantastic learning opportunity for me, because I got valuable exposure to clients and partners.

A month went by and I began to feel more 'senior' than my experience should have allowed. So, when the talk of a replacement SA came up, convinced that it was unnecessary and that I could handle the work, I told the SEM, 'Why can't I just do this? Why do you need a new SA?' I was sure she would be impressed that I was ready to take up more responsibility. Instead, she told me, politely and firmly, 'Radhika, you are good. But you are an analyst with two projects' worth of experience, not a senior associate. We need someone senior here.' Her words felt brutal. It was painful to swallow them, my ego was bruised, but today I understand they were not personal.

'No' is hard to hear, but hear it you will, especially if you have aspirations and ambition. But that shouldn't stop you from wanting or trying to do more and better. Years after this incident at McKinsey, dejected about a similar episode at another workplace, I wrote to one of my mentors about how frustrated I was. He left with me a line that has rushed back into my head every time I have heard a 'no' since. 'If there aren't times when you hear a "no", if there aren't days when you feel frustrated, if you don't feel pushed against the wall, then you are not aiming high enough.' He was right. Who has said that rejection is a badge of shame?

'IF THERE AREN'T TIMES WHEN YOU HEAR A "NO", IF THERE AREN'T DAYS WHEN YOU FEEL FRUSTRATED, IF YOU DON'T FEEL PUSHED AGAINST THE WALL, THEN YOU ARE NOT AIMING HIGH ENOUGH.'

On some of these 'no' days, when I'm feeling low, I find a friend in the stock market. Markets are fundamentally the business of creating wealth by taking risks, and the market can have big negative days, sometimes losing up to 5 per cent in a single day. And even though such days are a standard feature of markets and have occurred everywhere across the world since time immemorial, each

time there is a big fall the media has a field day.
Television screens are filled with red tickers,
anchors get agitated and announce the end of the
world and headlines scream
that billions of dollars of
market capitalization have
been wiped out in a single
day. The market corrects
once in a day, but a flurry of
headlines, tweets and WhatsApp messages among
multiple communities makes it feel like 10 cuts
have happened consecutively. Chances are, though,
that if you pick one of these days, and ask anyone
to recount its details even a year down the line, they
won't be able to do it. In the graph of market ups
and downs, such days are just data points that fade
with perspective.

ZOOM OUT. WHAT FEELS LIKE A BIG BLOT TODAY WILL BE A SMALL DOT TOMORROW.

Rejection is like that big 'down day' in equity
investing, an inevitable part of a game of taking
risks. When you face rejection of any kind, ask
yourself how much the incident – which feels like
the end of the world here and now – will matter
in five years. If you think about it, not that much.
Zoom out. What feels like a big blot today will be
a small dot tomorrow.

FEEDBACK: ACCEPT THE FRIEND REQUEST

'To avoid criticism, do nothing, say nothing, be nothing.'

– Elbert Hubbard

'YOU LACK EMOTIONAL MATURITY.'

These words stood out starkly in my second performance review at Edelweiss, shortly after Forefront was acquired. If the words sound cold on paper, they felt crushing in person. To be told something like this in a year in which I was delivering solid business results, well ahead of the targets assigned to me, made no sense. I was angry with myself, angry with my bosses, angry with the system. I was convinced that for some reason I was being targeted. Not for a minute did I believe what I had been told could be true.

Accepting difficult feedback gracefully is actually no different from having a sense of humour. We all believe we have the ability to handle criticism or a joke made at our expense, but few of us actually do. It's the reason performance review conversations are still some of the most awkward in most offices. Doling out tough truths is hard, and accepting them is even harder. This is why every review starts with the 'good stuff' first. In fact, after years of doing reviews, I have noticed that when the time comes to give 'critical' feedback, the body language of those being appraised quickly changes. They erect a shield to deflect the arrows even before any come their way.

There was nothing wrong with what I was told in my review. I have always been a sensitive person, and I was even more emotionally raw after five years at Forefront. All the signs were there. I got angry with people very quickly, I wrote long, defensive emails to channel partners who gave us feedback, and I had become legendary for being harsh and raising my voice at our vendors. My agitation came from an honest place – I think it was a manifestation of years of struggle as a young entrepreneur in India, a country I had hardly lived in earlier because I grew up across the world as a diplomat's daughter. No start-up has it easy and Forefront was no different. The day-to-day realities of setting up a business were brutal. I also felt constantly judged for my age in the asset management industry, where age is equated to wisdom and success. In the process, I developed a very reactive exterior. So much so that Nalin tacked on a post-it at my desk back then which said: 'DON'T BLOW UP'. As an entrepreneur, no one sits you down and gives you tough feedback, and a lot of the behaviour that is acceptable as a small-business owner definitely does not pass muster when you are a potential business leader in a large corporate set up. I was lucky that someone at Edelweiss not only told me this in a review but also worked with me later to correct it.

Tough criticism from the right people is a friend request you should not ignore.

Most consumer businesses measure a Net Promoter Score (NPS), usually done via surveys that ask clients to rate a product or a service on a scale of 1 to 10. They show up everywhere – when you exit Changi Airport in Singapore, after an Ola cab ride or once you complete most financial transactions.

TOUGH CRITICISM FROM THE RIGHT PEOPLE IS A FRIEND REQUEST YOU SHOULD NOT IGNORE.

For the business, customers who rate you highly (9–10) are your promoters, those who rate you poorly (1–6) are detractors, and the rest are your passives. NPS is calculated by subtracting the percentage of detractors from your promoters. At Edelweiss MF, we started measuring NPS a year after I joined, by calling our distribution partners, asking them a set of questions and recording the calls. The initial NPS surveys were negative (there were more detractors than promoters). The easiest thing to do when you don't like the results is to blame the survey process itself, and the immediate reaction when you see a bad score is to start defending yourself and blaming the distributor. I did all of this, until I realized that it would be a good idea to start listening to the detractor calls – that is, actually hear why they were rating us poorly. This proved to be an eye-opener for me. As it turned out, the so-called detractors were not ranting; they were taking out three, even five, minutes of their precious time to offer us feedback and tangible suggestions to improve. They were stating concrete reasons for their rating. They gave feedback on our products, our branches, our marketing collateral – this was real consumer feedback that would have been hard to come up with in strategy meets and executive reviews. As we listened to more calls, we understood what mattered in building the business, addressed the issue and, in time, saw our NPS turn positive.

All of us have a personal NPS, and improving it starts by listening to those 'detractor calls'. Tough feedback is not necessarily a sign that we are incompetent or disliked; it is often a statement that indicates we have a long way to go and that some people are ready to invest their time to help us get there. The feedback on emotional maturity was given to me by a former boss, who is one of the finest people leaders I have known, a young leader who rose to manage thousands of people within Edelweiss. Not only did he tell me this then, but over the years and through many conversations he also helped me work on these specific issues by sharing his own experiences and offering examples to help me better understand the point he was making.

TOUGH FEEDBACK IS NOT NECESSARILY A SIGN THAT WE ARE INCOMPETENT OR DISLIKED; IT IS OFTEN A STATEMENT THAT INDICATES WE HAVE A LONG WAY TO GO AND THAT SOME PEOPLE ARE READY TO INVEST THEIR TIME TO HELP US GET THERE.

Today, when I receive tough feedback, the first thing I ask myself is, 'How would it feel if my parents said this about me?' It helps me separate the critic and the criticism, and look at the contents more objectively.

Nine months before I delivered 'The Girl with a Broken Neck' at the GCS Connect platform, I delivered a version of that speech at a TEDx platform at Tata Institute of Social Sciences (TISS) in Mumbai. Captain Raghu Raman, former soldier, the CEO of the National Intelligence Grid (NATGRID) and a well-known speaker, whom I had first met during a training session at Edelweiss, was guiding me through the process. When I delivered the live talk at TISS, I sensed from the reactions of the audience that it had gone well, and I couldn't wait for it to release on YouTube. When the draft video was done, I sent it to Captain Raghu for feedback, pre-release. Forget liking the talk, his feedback was scathing: My voice had a staccato edge, my body language was a problem, and I had made the criminal mistake of wearing a black silk salwar suit when I had black hair and was speaking in front of a black background. 'You are looking like a moving black blob on the camera,' were his exact words. At first, I was upset and disappointed. But then I took a step back and broke down each of these points, and I realized he was right. As for the comment about wearing black, when I had made my first television appearance on *ET Now* in 2010, my mother had told me the same thing! If I could take it from her, why couldn't I listen when someone else said the same thing? That someone would bother to point out all of this to me with the same honesty that my mother would demonstrated just how much he cared.

There is, of course, a fine line between critical feedback and criticism for the sake of criticism, not to mention outright trolling. None of us is a stranger to trolling online and offline (who doesn't have that one relative who has to have an opinion on everything from our weight to our career choices?). If I was to make a distinction I'd say trolling is malicious, while feedback is constructive, thought through and actionable.

In Disney's *Ratatouille*, the main character, Remy, a rat who is a master chef, finds himself up against Anton Ego, an acerbic food critic, whose reviews have killed many a restaurant and career. Ego is a man whose criticism comes from not 'liking food, but loving it so much that he doesn't eat bad food', explaining his stick-thin figure. He chases excellence, and pushes Remy to do so too – becoming his biggest supporter and patron by the end of the film. Both my boss who cautioned me about my lack of emotional maturity and Captain Raghu have given me some of the toughest feedback I have received (and they continue to do so without so much as batting an eyelid). Consequently, much of what I know about leadership comes from the former and everything I know about storytelling comes from Captain Raghu.

After my TEDx fiasco, when I was rationalizing with Captain Raghu, telling him the audience liked the talk that he was being so critical of, he reminded me politely that the talk didn't appear impactful on video, even if I felt it had been effective in person. 'And, Radhika, if your standard is a 9 on 10, this is a 3 or 4. I know it, and you do too.' The quest for excellence pushes you hard, and everyone needs their own circle of critics who come from a positive and caring place. Today I am glad I heard him out and finally never released the TEDx TISS video.

Most of us have been in a situation in which someone has told us, 'I have two pieces of news for you, one good and one bad. Which one do you want to hear first?' Research says that 75 per cent of us prefer to hear the bad news first. Listening to tough news quickly can help us course correct when the stakes are low and prevent costly mistakes when the stakes are higher. As Captain Raghu has said in a segment on Josh Talks, 'It is better to have misfires on the training ground than [to have them] in the battlefield.' In 2018, just after becoming CEO, a senior colleague told me that I was perceived by my team as being biased. As a leader, this is one of the worst things you can be told. I had a long argument with him and explained that this was probably because I was focusing on certain parts of the business that were new to me. He said that there was more to it than that, and I should count how many casual conversations I had daily with people from different departments and how I reacted to emails from different teams. 'Ask yourself, why would anyone believe you are biased? Stop thinking about reality, and ask yourself whether the perception is true. What would it mean for you as a leader?' It was a bitter pill to swallow, but I am glad I got a serving of it in the early phase of building my team. A leader has to behave, and also appear to behave, in an unbiased manner. Today, in any situation that involves conflict resolution, I do a mental check for any bias on my part and ask myself if I am being and appearing to be fair.

While growing up, for some time I studied in Rome. My high school there, Marymount International School, had a year-end assembly where the school honoured two students from each grade in every subject. One award was given to the 'Best Student' and the second to the 'Most Improved Student', the one who had taken her or his teacher's feedback and made real strides during the year. I have to admit that back then, with my Type A personality, I never understood the need for the 'Most Improved' category. Now I understand why it matters. Each of us is a work in progress, and stars are awarded to those willing to improve and be a better version of themselves.

Three years after the TEDx TISS incident, Captain Raghu visited my office and among the pictures on my cabin wall he noticed a picture of a certificate from TEDx TISS.

'Why do you have this here when the talk was never released?' he asked me.

I reminded him of the feedback he had given me and how I felt when I heard it. 'That single incident taught me that I need to think through the tiniest details of how I present myself, including what I wear, when I step on stage.' To me, that certificate – despite the talk never making it to YouTube – is as powerful as the other awards it shares space with.

One of the most telling examples of the power of feedback I have heard is from Rashesh Shah, managing director (MD) and CEO of Edelweiss. Unsurprisingly, it drew on the stock market.

The market, through all its participants, gives live feedback on companies every day, which is what the stock prices represent. Rashesh revealed that he does an exercise that involves him looking at the maximum fall a company's

BUILDING A RESILIENT CAREER IS NOT VERY DIFFERENT FROM BUILDING A ROBUST COMPANY. WHEN FEEDBACK AND CRITICISM SEND YOU THAT FRIEND REQUEST, ACCEPT IT WITH OPEN ARMS.

stock experiences in deep market crises and how the extent of that fall changes with time. The stocks of Kotak Mahindra Bank, for instance, fell over 70 per cent during the 2008 crisis. In the 2013 correction, however, the fall was less than 30 per cent and subsequent falls have also been less sharp even in deep market corrections like the one that happened in 2020. As Rashesh puts it, this proves that with time winning companies like Kotak Mahindra get more robust, because when they fall sharply they take feedback and use it to get stronger and better at what they do. It is feedback that helps them build this powerful, almost Teflon-like coating.

Building a resilient career is not very different from building a robust company. When feedback and criticism send you that friend request, accept it with open arms.

RE-DIRECTION:
CONNECT THE BRIDGE

'A bend in the road is not the end of the road...
Unless you fail to make the turn.'

– Hellen Keller

I HAVE ALWAYS WANTED TO SING. I JUST HAPPEN TO be a terrible singer (my brother says I sound like a frog).

When I was a teenager, while we lived in Nigeria, at the American school I attended there, popularity was not defined by grades but by extracurricular activities. This boiled down to music and athletics. My athletic skills are worse than my musical ability, so I abandoned sports pretty quickly, but decided I would conquer music by working hard enough. I signed up for piano classes and took part in the choir with all my friends (who happened to be exceptionally good singers) and, even though I had received enough signals that I wasn't particularly good, I auditioned for our school play that year – *Bye Bye Birdie*. The lead in it had to sing through the entire play. 'I am going to work so hard that I will make up for my voice,' I told myself. When I was (obviously!) rejected in the audition, one of the judges mentioned that while I didn't quite cut it as a singer, I had a strong voice that could lend itself well to speaking on stage, debating and plays. I dismissed this as a polite consolation prize. Rejected by music, I turned to playing Bridge, a game of cards my parents played and taught us because it was a convenient way to entertain two children in a country where you could not step out after 6 p.m. due to security reasons.

Cut to eight years later. After the seven straight rejections at UPenn and getting through the crisis that followed, I moved on to my eighth and final consulting interview with McKinsey, the biggest name in the business. At that meeting I happened to be interviewed by someone who was a passionate Bridge player and had never met a person who had played the game from the age of 13. Eighty-five minutes of our 90-minute conversation ended up being about the card game, and I got that consulting job – in part because I ticked all the usual boxes of grades and pedigree, and partly because of my unusual hobby. Back to my lack of musical prowess, today, if there is one thing I love doing outside of work it is public speaking, and I am told that my voice is one of my stronger points on stage. Who would have imagined?

In his now legendary commencement speech at Stanford University in 2005, Steve Jobs told all of us, 'You can't connect the dots looking forward; you can only connect them looking behind. You have to trust that the dots will connect in the future.' Life's dots connect in ways we can't ever decipher, so how can we expect to determine the way it will happen? Yes, I did get a signal about the strength of my voice, but I would never have believed it if I was told that one day I would land a job I was desperately seeking thanks to a game I picked up to pass time when I had nothing else to do.

If you visit a career counsellor, they will present you with a chart that says your ideal career is the meeting point of four circles in a Venn diagram – what you like, what you are good at, what the world needs and what you will be paid for. That tiny middle point, where the circles interact, has a small star, and that is your destination, your ideal career, your purpose. A Venn diagram looks very neat on a chart, but rarely does real life reflect that neatness.

As children, we are constantly asked what our favourite subject is, and the answer to that question is eventually meant to box us into a career. I was one of those kids who didn't have a favourite subject; I did everything but loved nothing in particular. I chose a joint degree programme at UPenn because I could study both computer science and economics, and defer making a choice. Two years into the programme, I had interned at Microsoft with a classmate named Bertan Aygun. Studying and working closely with him made one thing very clear to me – that Bertan and I were very different. He was tickled by the idea of debugging code and could spend night after night reading about operating systems. I was not that person; I liked software, but not enough to want to spend my life being a developer. Consulting was my attempt at finding a more generalist role.

A year into the analyst programme at McKinsey, however, I realized that consulting was too broad an area. I wanted to go back to an operating business. Like Goldilocks trying to identify the chair that was 'just right', the next thing I tried was asset management at AQR. In 2009, when I started Forefront, my partners (Nalin, who until then worked at Goldman Sachs, and Anant Jatia, a colleague from AQR) and I quickly realized that there was a lot more to running a business – marketing, compliance, HR and administration – than mere knowledge of the sector. Since we couldn't afford employees, one of the founders had to take on the role of managing all the 'other stuff'. This role came to me. The boys nudged me on to don the mantle, and I put it on happily, because I realized that just as I didn't want to spend all my life writing code, I didn't want to spend it researching stocks either. So I threw myself into doing everything – tracking down distributors, dealing with the regulator, and even making accounting entries on Tally and creating vouchers. I learnt how to network with journalists on LinkedIn to get media visibility and how to get top-notch slots during the IIT Bombay placement season, despite being a start-up.

By the time Edelweiss acquired our business in 2014, my experience running it qualified me to work as a 'business head' rather than a functionally focused asset manager. Doing the 'other stuff' gave me direction and eventually defined the course of my career. Years after the Forefront acquisition in 2014, when Edelweiss decided to focus on expanding the mutual fund business in 2017, I happened to have enough fund management and business experience to take on the role of CEO. Today, I am doing a job that I love – one that is a mix of big-picture thinking and hands-on execution. Plus, it has enough facets to keep me interested, given my love for variety. After a few trysts with rejection and a whole lot of confusion, a decade into my career, I have found a space that is 'just right'.

Vinati Saraf Mutreja, MD and CEO of Vinati Organics, one of India's fastest-growing chemical companies (declared as one of the biggest wealth creators of the 2010–20 decade), who was also my classmate in college, says that careers are a combination of 'choices and chances'. That is my story – unexpected rejections, some conscious and some forced choices, and a few chances that I have tried to make the most of. It has been her story as well. She studied chemical engineering when everyone was obsessed with computer science and finance, and joined her father to run a ₹20-crore market cap company, with one severely loss-making unit. A lot of hard work and some good choices later, she is the CEO of a company that has a ₹20,000-crore market cap.

When faced with a decision on your choice of career, I can only say this: Do not rush to fill in the star in your Venn diagram. Discover it.

It is absolutely normal to be confused, to not understand what you would like to do with your life as you grow up. Lines like 'find your passion' and 'fall in love' sound great on paper, but what if these things don't happen in reality? What if you don't discover your passion, or cannot pursue your passion because of sheer bad luck? In the same way that those of us in India who don't discover love have arranged marriages, which often turn out to be very successful, some of us have 'arranged careers' that work brilliantly for us.

My father is a gold medallist in botany, and wanted to join the Indian Forest Service, but while he cleared the written exam, he was rejected outright because of his atrocious eyesight. He ended up joining the Indian Foreign Service, and hasn't regretted it for a single a day. C.K. Venkataraman, MD and CEO of Titan, once admitted in a conversation with *Business Standard* that he had fancied being a *National Geographic* photographer in a jungle, but ended up spending 30 years in the retail business. He said, 'I learnt to love what I did and stopped chasing what I loved.'[1] So do not feel pressured to find the right opportunity. Take the opportunities you have, and make them the right ones for you.

Date, get engaged, have your heart broken, and you will, albeit perhaps a little late, find a career you want to live with and hopefully love.

The other factor that will help you understand what you are good at is time. Our perceptions of our strengths and weaknesses are shaped largely by our functional abilities early on in our careers, because we have little exposure to 'soft skills' like creativity, leadership and dealing with ambiguity. The definition of what you are good at is also relative as the bar rises from school to college to the workplace; every high schooler who is good at physics is not cut out to be a physicist. Rejection and tough feedback will help you chisel out these answers. For many of us, the original

> **DO NOT FEEL PRESSURED TO FIND THE RIGHT OPPORTUNITY. TAKE THE OPPORTUNITIES YOU HAVE, AND MAKE THEM THE RIGHT ONES FOR YOU.**

---

[1] Pavan Lall, 'I learnt to love what I did and stopped chasing what I loved: Titan MD', *Business Standard*, 21 November 2020.

choice of career could be based on what we like and feel we are good at, or it could be shaped by family pressure, and in some cases by our not being aware of the choices and alternatives. I know this because coming from a background where no one I knew personally was in the corporate world (in our *sarkari* world we called it 'private sector'), I had very little idea about different career paths even when I graduated.

It is also important to remember in your winding journey that every experience you have, while it may not relate to your current role, will add something to your résumé. You never know which one will be your game of Bridge. In late 2020, at a time when we were rolling out transformational digital projects at Edelweiss MF, I was left to run our business without a senior chief technology officer (CTO) for a brief period and I ended up spending a lot of time with our technology teams. I hadn't written a line of code since college, 20 years ago, but my computer science degree and stint at Microsoft had armed me with the knowledge of tech speak, which came in handy and gave me the confidence I needed to get through.

Subconsciously, all of us are shaped by the idea that there is only one right choice. In campuses, it is the 'Day 0 company', the one that comes to recruit on the first day, because the students and the placement cell nominate them as the most desirable place to work. Being the Day 0 company is a matter of prestige and campuses have their reasons for their pick. For each of us though there is a different Day 0 company, a different 'good' 'right choice', a different fit. In a talk from 2019 at TEDxYouth@ HFSI, ad genius Prahlad Kakkar says that every individual needs to find their own 'north star', and that star is defined by the process of discovery. It is not very different from the star in the Venn diagram and is entirely your own – not defined by your parents, your neighbours and friends.

One of my favourite characters from a book is the Cheshire Cat in Lewis Carroll's *Alice in Wonderland*. Known for his creepy and distinctive grin, he is a guiding spirit for Alice, directing her to the March Hare's house and the mad tea party, and ultimately towards the garden, her final star. This is one of their more memorable conversations.

Alice: Which way do I go?

Cheshire Cat: That depends a good deal on where you want to get to.

Alice: I don't care much where, as long as I get somewhere.

Cheshire Cat: Oh, you're sure to do that. As long as you walk long enough.

You may fall, and you may fail, but consider rejections to be your Cheshire Cat. They will give you signals and if you listen to them with an open mind you can redirect yourself to a place that is meant for you. Be open about your destination and remember that the dots will connect, and sometimes even conspire, to make you succeed – just as long as you don't stop walking.

TAKING RISKS, UNDER-STANDING SIPS AND SURVIVING BLIPS

RISK: REMEMBER THAT RETURNS ARE NOT FREE

'If no one ever took risks, Michelangelo would have painted the Sistine floor.'

– Neil Simon

MOST OF US, AT SOME POINT IN OUR LIVES, HAVE BEEN told that to be 'well-settled' is our ultimate goal. It's a uniquely Indian phrase for all the boxes we have to check to achieve such a status – starting with a good education, continued with a comfortable, well-paying job with a big brand, followed by a socially acceptable wedding and of course children a few years later. Then come the car and the house… And the list goes on.

I've often wondered what being 'well-settled' really means. It has the distinct smell of a comfort zone, but one that is defined by someone else. It feels like a box that you enter but can't exit, because you have everything that 'matters' – to someone else. In a world of unbounded opportunities, focusing on being well-settled binds your aspirations. I know the temptation to chase the feeling. When I went abroad for college in 2001 – the first in my family to do so – an Ivy League education cost $40,000 a year, aggregating over four years to ₹1 crore in Indian currency. My father's salary couldn't fund a fraction of that cost, but I received a substantial financial aid which enabled me to complete the course (that story comes later). My fellow Indian classmates were full-fee paying children of industrialists, and while money is always relative I was perennially conscious of being the least well-to-do entrant from India in my UPenn class, the one who worked three jobs to earn $8 an hour, bought cheap second-hand textbooks and avoided taking trips with friends.

At the end of my second year at UPenn, I received an offer for an internship from Microsoft in Seattle and immediately called my parents to give them the news. When I told them I was going to be paid $5,000 a month, my parents were shocked that a 19-year-old, after only two years of college education, was going to make more money than my father had at the peak of his career. (Incidentally, my 15-minute call ended up costing me $150, which taught me that making international calls from a hotel room was a very bad idea indeed!)

After I joined McKinsey two years later, I began enjoying all the perks that young consultants get – fancy hotel rooms, room service and business-class travel. It got even better when I joined Wall Street during the 2006–07 boom. Shortly after joining AQR, I once went for lunch with an ex-colleague from McKinsey, and, at the end of the meal, she stared at my black handbag – a $10 piece I had bought in 2005 and was quite proud of – and asked me why I was carrying such a cheap-looking bag when I worked as a hedge fund manager. 'Go buy a Louis Vuitton, girl,' she told me. Clueless about the world of handbags, but brimming with confidence that I could afford it, I asked her for the address of a showroom for the brand. Two hours later, I walked out with a $1,400 bag in my hand. My extended family remained shocked for years at the price of my handbag. Well before *Zindagi Na Milegi Dobara* had made buying an expensive handbag an event, I had lived a 'Bagwati' moment of my own.

Material success can be very heady, especially when you've grown up with middle-class values.

**NO MATTER HOW
BIG A BRAND YOU
WORK FOR, HOW
GLAMOROUS YOUR
INDUSTRY, OR HOW
BIG YOUR CORNER
OFFICE, RISK ALWAYS
EXISTS.**

There is something about ordering room service on your own money when for years, on family vacations, you've eaten aloo–poori packed by your mother. 'I can finally afford this,' you tell yourself, and it feels good. However, the flip side is that it becomes hard to take risks that may upset your 'well-settled' state. And so we stay on in jobs that we stopped enjoying many years ago, dream of starting a business but never take the plunge because of the lure of a monthly pay cheque, and give up a bigger role at a young company because it's safer to work at the more established one.

But no matter how big a brand you work for, how glamorous your industry, or how big your corner office, risk always exists. I learnt how risk can suddenly appear right in your face, without you realizing it, when the Wall Street boom made way for the disaster of 2008. The turn started when Bear Stearns collapsed in March that year, but the final nail on the coffin was driven in on the night of my twenty-fifth birthday, 14 September 2008, when Lehman Brothers went under. As uncertainty loomed over the careers and lives of pretty much everyone in the financial sector, the atmosphere in the office gradually changed and over the next few months tempers flared more often than not. A new word – 'lay off' – could be heard in all the corridor conversations. When would it happen, who would be the victims, what would be the terms? Would it just be one round or two? Every person wondered if it would be them. For those of us living in the US on employer-sponsored visas, the thought of a pink slip and an immediate return home was even scarier.

The 'lay-off day' at my workplace finally came, and it still ranks as one of the darkest days I have seen in my career. I saw close friends, sitting at desks a few feet away from me, getting the fateful call; their computer screens went blank and within minutes they were walked out of the office, carrying their belongings stuffed in plastic bags. Careers that had been built over three, five, seven years ended in less than seven minutes. For many of us who lived through 2008, the most haunting memory we carry is not the economic loss, not the portfolios that folded, not the stock market crash, but the sinking and miserable feeling of seeing colleagues lose their jobs for reasons completely beyond their control. We had studied at the best schools in the world, we earned big bonuses for our age, and then we became the ultimate victims of a 'black swan' (read Nassim Nicholas Taleb's book with that name to know more!). That year taught me that life is uncertain, that circumstances can arise out of nowhere and knock you over. In the fourteen years since then, I have seen many more careers abruptly being hit by adverse incidents – an MNC shutting down its India operations because of a global directive, inter-company mergers leading to a set of people becoming redundant, restructuring because of economic conditions, or an older CEO losing her job to a younger one.

Seeing life unravel in 2008 gave me the courage to finally take a risk and move back to India to start Forefront, my own asset management company. It pushed me into giving up a dollar salary and a New Yorker's lifestyle and move to a life of zero assured income, embracing the status of a struggling entrepreneur.

Taking risks is not easy. It is not nearly as romantic as books and movies make it out to be. 'Risk *hai to ishq hai*' sounds far better in the reel world of *Scam 1992* than it does in real life, and there is much more to living a start-up life than the glamorous rapid-fire pitches on shows like *Shark Tank*. While taking risks can be hard for an individual, it is often even harder for the family. My parents were not the happiest people when I told them about my plan to move back, and I don't blame them. Who wants a child who is 'well-settled', after years of collective struggle to make it happen for her, to plunge back into a world of uncertainty? At first, they gently dissuaded me, even suggesting that my partners and I wait a few years before making the move, or try to return as employees of a large financial services company in India. What helped then, and has helped each time I have thought of taking risks, was assessing the worst-case outcome – the ultimate back-up plan. I would keep asking Nalin, 'What if it fails?' And he'd say, 'We're young, we have savings, we can get an MBA degree and start again.' Fortunately, we never had to exercise that option, but having it at hand gave us immense confidence.

Risk is less intimidating when we rationalize it in our minds and then, if needed, with those close to us. Ask yourself what you really have to lose and what you can possibly gain. Then, as we say at Edelweiss, ask yourself if you can afford the former and if the latter is worth it.

One of my favourite conversations about taking risks sensibly has been with Dr Arokiaswamy Velumani, the founder and MD of Thyrocare, one of India's largest diagnostics companies. He went from having just ₹500 in his pocket to seeing an idea grow into a listed company with a ₹5,000-crore market cap and he calls his journey a 'romance with risk'. Behind his punchline, however, is a thought-out approach to risk-taking. When Dr Velumani left his government job to start his enterprise, he was comforted by the fact that his wife worked at the State Bank of India and that there was at least one steady salary that would run the home. When he told her he had quit, she decided to leave her job and join the business with him. Noticing that he was surprised at her response she reminded him to think of the worst-case scenario. 'There are so many boarding schools in educational towns like Panchgani. I will always get a job as a principal because I have a PhD. You can become my secretary,' she told him. With this reassurance, his savings of ₹2 lakh, a substantial sum in the late 1990s, and the knowledge that he had no financial liabilities to plan for, Dr Velumani was ready to embark on the start-up journey. In a sense, he took a sensible risk – he reached for the upside after assessing the downsides and ticking off a few important boxes.

I have had many conversations with friends from the corporate world looking to take their big plunge into entrepreneurship, and their common worry, beyond disrupting a well-settled lifestyle, is the weight of reputation. They all seem to worry whether in their new, unpredictable venture they will be able to live up to the name they have created for themselves through their exemplary education, stellar career and the weighty title on their business card. Mihir A. Desai, economist and professor of finance at Harvard Business School, addressed this well in an essay he wrote for the *Harvard Crimson*, the daily student newspaper of the university. He says new graduates have the tendency to 'collect options', the proverbial move 'from being a Yale undergraduate, to going to work for McKinsey for two years, then going to Harvard Business School, then graduating and going to Goldman Sachs, and then several years later working for Blackstone.'[1] This tendency, along with the comfort of a high-paying job, becomes so addictive that it kills the ability to take meaningful risks. A Yale, a

---

[1] Mihir A. Desai, 'The Trouble with Optionality', *The Harvard Crimson*, 25 May 2017.

McKinsey or a Goldman Sachs admits you for your extraordinary potential but, in the end, without seizing unique opportunities and taking those chances beyond the formulaic, that potential never gets realized, and the dreams that the 'options' could have enabled recede into the background.

This is not just true for new graduates; the effect compounds as we collect more labels and brands to add to our résumés. By all means, be grateful for the education you have received and the companies you have worked for. Strong educational backgrounds and work experience do give you a valuable foundation and a market reputation, and we should all aspire for the best we can access and afford. But, in aspiring for and collecting pedigree, do not let yourself become imprisoned by it.

There are various degrees of risk-taking, and they don't necessarily involve starting a business. You can take risks in the context of being an employee, by working for a younger company in your industry or working with an unproven leader – opportunities where the probability of success may be less certain. Even today, there is tremendous inertia among a lot of people to move beyond the comfort of an established brand. I got a taste of this when I was hiring for Edelweiss MF in 2017, just after taking over as CEO. We were a young Indian brand, ranked twenty-sixth in our industry, with a small team, and we were struggling to hire salespeople in Mumbai. In a bid to help my team, I said I would front the interview process, hoping more people would show up to meet the CEO. Our HR team had set up a roster at the offices of the Mumbai Cricket Association (MCA) in the Bandra Kurla Complex located near our office and I made my way there prepared for a full day of candidate interviews. The first interview was scheduled for 10 a.m. The candidate didn't show up. The second one was scheduled for 11 a.m. The candidate didn't show up. This happened back-to-back over six interview slots. Indignant that no one had turned up even though they had confirmed their attendance in advance and knew they were to meet the CEO, I asked my team what had gone wrong. The HR team's response was, 'It's not easy to hire when you aren't a big brand.' It's true that small brands come with their chaos and uncertainty, I told my HR team, but they also give an individual a chance to contribute, learn and grow disproportionately. And when the risk pays off, the individual gets disproportionate credit versus his counterpart at a larger brand.

WHEN WE LOOK AT SUCCESSFUL PROFESSIONALS WE ADMIRE, WE OFTEN FORGET THAT THEY ARE ALSO A RESULT OF SMART RISK-TAKING.

When we look at successful professionals we admire, we often forget that they are also a result of smart risk-taking. A fund manager I once interviewed asked me why he could not have the kind of compensation that Neelesh Surana, the chief investment officer (CIO) of Mirae Mutual Fund and one of India's most successful asset managers, received. While Neelesh is an exceptional money manager, he also joined Mirae in 2008 when they were an unknown brand with hardly any assets. He grew the brand to become one of India's most successful equity fund houses and he grew with the brand; he took a risk and was compensated for it. There are countless such stories.

When you take risks, you may not make the money your peers do in the early stages, but you often take on larger roles, and if you perform well, you are compensated handsomely later. I have seen so many folks at larger brands, who keep collecting salaries without significant growth in their roles, and eventually become redundant or overpriced for the role. The first strategy appears risky, the second one has hidden tail risks.

At the heart of finance are two instruments – stocks and bonds. Bonds are safe. They pay you a fixed rate of interest in the form of periodic coupons. Think of the quarterly interest on your fixed deposits and you will know what I am saying. Stocks are volatile and unpredictable, and they have inherent risk. But they can and do create real wealth over the long term. Do not build your career like a bond and be satisfied with collecting predictable coupons, because as much as I love bonds their upside is capped. It is stocks that make for the exciting stories.

Speaking of excitement, do you remember when Ranbir Kapoor's character Bunny in *Yeh Jawaani Hai Deewani*, an almost compulsive traveller on a mission to see the world, tells Deepika Padukone's character Naina that he wants his life to be a constant set of discoveries? *'Main udna chahta hoon, daudna chahta hoon, girna bhi chahta hoon. Bas theherna nahi chahta.'* I want to fly, I want to run, I want to fall. But I don't want to stop. That is a great career in a line, one that steps out of the safe zone and takes a few risks, one that maximizes the myriad of opportunities out there, and one that is not well-settled, but well-travelled.

SMALL IS POWERFUL (SIP): GET STARTED

'You don't have to see the whole staircase. Just take the first step.'

— Martin Luther King

WHEN I WAS IN MY SECOND YEAR AT UPENN, ONE of my closest friends and I had applied for an internship programme with a prominent bank and were rejected. We were both angry and decided we needed a way to channel our energy into activities or enterprises outside of our classes. For months, we had dreamt about starting a small business together, and we now began discussing it seriously. The first thing that came to our minds was that it should be something related to food. Neither of us was a great cook, though we did cook occasionally to satisfy our cravings and to take a break from the tasteless naan and paneer tikka served in the Indian restaurants on campus. Home-cooked food was a rare find on campus and our friends frequently took away whatever we made, so we finally landed upon the idea of starting a restaurant. We decided it would be run out of our dorm and serve simple, home-cooked meals.

'Let's just start it. Now. Why not now?' My friend urged me one afternoon.

I didn't have a great answer to her question. So we called our respective mothers, and figured out what two novices could cook in a limited dorm room kitchen with three little hot plates passing off as a stove. My roommate was a Hyderabadi, so she had the non-vegetarian items checked off, and being a Delhi–Uttar Pradesh girl I took on the paneer-and-chapati kind of meals. We decided we would price our food at $5 for a vegetarian plate and $6 for the non-vegetarian one. We would sell the meals from 10 p.m. to 2 a.m. because the only competition we would have during that time was the pizza delivered to the college by the likes of Domino's and Papa John's.

With all this planning in the bag, we started telling our Indian friends about our new business idea, excited about spreading the word among a bunch of hungry prospective customers. The response surprised us. Overwhelmingly, the single question we were asked was, 'What is your business plan?' There were other questions too: What was our revenue model? When would we break even? Would we capitalize or expense the assets? Did we have a marketing strategy? Would anyone buy from us, and why?

We had no answers to any of these questions. In fact, we hadn't even thought about half of them. Fortunately, though I may have been inclined to give up, my roommate certainly wasn't. She came up with an idea, 'Let's not try to sell anything on the first day. Let's just deliver free food to all our prospective customers.' So that's what we did. We packed little styrofoam containers with dal, sabzi, chapati, dahi and pickles, wrapped them in foil and made the deliveries. Free home-cooked Indian food, delivered at students' doorsteps, at 10 p.m. The next day, we cooked again and then packed some more containers. But this time we had buyers at our door. As our customer base grew, our food became better tasting and better looking as we incorporated the generous doses of ideas and advice we received from our mothers. Before we knew it, our little venture, which we christened Mirch Madness (a spicy take on the US intercollege basketball tournament March Madness), was in business. My first business thus took off because one random day my roommate and I had the courage to make a start.

We've all heard that Rome was not built in a day, but as James Clear writes in his book *Atomic Habits*, 'You build an empire by laying a brick.'[2] Unfortunately, for

TAKING RISKS IS OFTEN ABOUT TAKING THE FIRST SMALL STEP AND SIMPLY GETTING STARTED.

most of us setting out to embark on something new, more time is usually spent discussing the building of the empire than on simply laying the bricks. After all, empire-building is exciting to visualize and discuss, while laying bricks is hard, unglamorous work. But the truth is, taking risks is often about taking the first small step and simply getting started.

Both business schools and boardrooms train us to focus on the big picture, but in reality making a beginning, however small, is the most critical part. Getting started ensures we have skin in the game and forces us to deal with problems head on. It is when you make a start that you also make real mistakes (not just theoretical ones) and quickly

---

[2] James Clear, *Atomic Ideas: An Easy & Proven Way to Build Good Habits & Break Bad Ones*, Avery: New York, 2018.

learn to course correct. It is when you make a start that you learn what you don't know and who you need to know. Businesses are not born from plans chalked out on an Excel sheet, but from facing the real grind and challenges on the battlefield.

In the money-management business, how much money you manage, your assets under management (AUM), is the most important metric of success. All asset managers aspire to manage billions of dollars of AUM. But in May 2009, when Nalin, Anant and I started Forefront, the only thing on our minds was to get a company up and running. We were three 24-year-olds who had just quit their jobs and were full of enthusiasm, and it was important that we felt like we were accomplishing something every few weeks. In the first month, it was about creating a company and getting approvals from the Registrar of Companies. In the second, it was drafting an application to the Securities and Exchange Board of India (SEBI), the securities regulator (we drafted the 60-page document ourselves because we could not afford a lawyer). In the third month, we learnt everything about running the back office of an asset-management business and coded what became our reporting platform. Every accomplishment felt good, from getting a PAN card to finally getting our Portfolio Management Services (PMS) license from SEBI. We built the company brick by brick, and in September of that year Forefront was ready for business. We approached every family member, friend, family friend and friend of a friend to start raising money. Finally, we started with ₹25 lakh of AUM from a single client, the legal minimum SEBI allowed businesses to start with. If there is something called a small start, this was it.

After six months of being in business, we had collected a measly sum of ₹2 crore of AUM. But we kept at it – 2 crore grew to 20, and 20 to 200, which was the AUM we were handling when we sold the business to Edelweiss. A few years from its inception, as the business started growing, a number of aspiring start-up asset management firms began to come by and ask us for advice. Everyone we met was intelligent, had rock-solid credentials and was raring to go. But you could clearly divide them into two groups. On the one hand was the group that talked about big game plans (think $100 million AUMs) and the depth of their connections. On the other hand was the one that was equally ambitious about building big, but also wanted concrete advice on the basics of building the business: how to deal with regulators, connect with distributors and efficiently set up a back office. A few years later, it became evident that it was the second group, the one interested in getting a foundation in place, that had got off the ground. Not talking about building an empire doesn't mean you want it any less; it just means you choose to focus on the process of getting started, rather than concentrating on the outcome.

Execution is a very effective teacher. As for us, six months into our business, after targeting all the obvious friends-and-family clients, we realized that Forefront had no visibility or brand. We learnt how to build both. A year into the business, we also understood that three people hunting by themselves for rich individuals to give them money to manage is not a sustainable business model in India. We needed to find banks, wealth managers and distributors of financial products who would enable us to reach more people and share the economics with them. Two years and many client meetings and rejections later, we learnt that our products, which were a function of our training in the US, were fundamentally too complex for the Indian market, which is perhaps why we had struggled so much with fundraising in the beginning. We learnt how to build much simpler products, and in fact, I believe, the first truly good product we launched was in 2013. Each of these learnings came about because we had the courage to make a start, and then play the game with real money – not paper money.

RISK-TAKING IS DAUNTING AND HAVING SHORT-TERM TARGETS MAKES IT FEEL LESS SO. FOCUSING ON TAKING INCREMENTAL SMALL STEPS GIVES US THE OPPORTUNITY TO CELEBRATE THE SMALL MILESTONES.

The journey of climbing a mountain from its base to 10,000 feet is never achieved in a single step. You move from 0 to 500 feet and it is only at 500 feet that you have the ability to see the 1,000-feet milestone. At that milestone, a little more confidence sets in and you make your way to 2,000 feet and then to 5,000 feet. And when you are finally there, you can make a real attempt to climb to 10,000 feet. But it all starts with conquering those first steps, starting from zero.

I would never say long-term vision is not important, but it has to be coupled with short-term execution – this is what Rashesh calls bi-focal vision. Risk-taking is daunting and having short-term targets makes it feel doable.

I am surrounded by runners both at home and at Edelweiss. Every runner, including my husband Nalin, will tell you that you don't complete a marathon by running 42 kilometres, you run one kilometre at a time, 42 times. Nalin completed the Ironman triathlon in 2021, an athletic feat that involves swimming for about 4 kilometres, cycling for 180 kilometres and then running for 42 kilometres – all of this back-to-back and within a set time. It is audacious stuff. As Nalin puts it, it is the equivalent of swimming from Navy Nagar, at the tip of Mumbai, to the Gateway of India, then cycling from Mumbai to Pune, and then doing a full marathon – all at a stretch. When most people see Nalin today, they assume he has been a champion athlete for a long time. They're surprised when I tell them that till 2016 he had a happy Indian belly and didn't know what the Ironman challenge entailed. One day, he took the decision to work on his fitness and signed up for the Mumbai half-marathon, with the sole objective of finishing it, which he did by walking most of the 21 kilometres. His next goal was to complete the half-marathon without walking for any length of it, and the next was running 21 kilometres every month. Months later, he finished his first full marathon in Berlin, but as his running experience grew he realized he wasn't going to get much further till he worked on his nutrition. His diet underwent a makeover, and his passion for running translated into swimming classes and cycling, and finally the Ironman. But it all started with that clunky, imperfect start of walking that first half-marathon.

Focusing on taking incremental small steps also gives us the opportunity to celebrate the small milestones. I learnt the real power of this from Deepak Jain, who heads sales at Edelweiss MF, and joined us very early in our journey from a significantly larger asset management company. Selling systematic investment plans (SIPs) is an important part of our business, and when Deepak started in 2018, we were adding a very embarrassing 400 SIPs a month. I had told him with great pride that our Kolkata branch had a target of 100 SIPs, and much later, in 2021, he told me how much he had resisted the urge to laugh at me back then. Deepak set a target for our sales team to hit 10,000 SIPs a month, which was audacious at the very least. But he divided the journey of achieving the 10,000 SIPs into smaller milestones each week and sometimes each day (he named these the 'mega login days'). On the WhatsApp group we have for our all-India team, we cheered and celebrated every time 20 or 50 SIPs were logged in. I found this strange, because in themselves the additions were very small, and it felt like we were always celebrating something. But celebrating small achievements mattered to the salespeople on the field and one person's success usually gave the 80 others in the team the energy to fight another day. Deepak often tells me that what we call routine business, going out and selling our product every day, can be very boring, but there is no other way to build the business. Decorating the long journey of small steps with little celebrations makes it more endurable. Incidentally, with 10,000 and 25,000 SIPs a month in our bag, Deepak is now laying a plan to get to 50,000 and 1,00,000 SIPs.

Which brings me to the most successful thing my industry has created – the concept of the SIP itself. SIPs push you to continually invest small amounts every month and I have always believed that they are never about the return on investment. They work because of the habit they drive – they allow you to start investing very humble amounts and ensure you do it consistently. Over time, you build a corpus that is meaningful and investors are often surprised at how far this gradual habit carries them. Before they know it, a few thousand rupees in an SIP done every month funds a child's education expenses or a dream home. As I tell young investors who seek investment advice, sometimes it is better to stop overthinking investing – the fund, the amount, and the idea – and just get started. The rest falls into place along the way. If you apply this to your career, the lesson is just as clear and strong – don't be afraid to start your journey of risk-taking with a humble beginning and let it build into something meaningful, just like an SIP.

In his book *Tales from My Heart,* Ruskin Bond writes that even the great act of discovering America could not be done with just inspiration and ideas. America had always existed, 'but it was discovered only when the ocean had been crossed. And [to do that] someone had to build the ship. And know how to sail it.'[3] Taking risks is a journey of discovery, and it begins with a thousand questions, some internal and some external. The good thing is – as that afternoon before Mirch Madness took off taught me – you don't need all the answers to embark on it. You just need to go out there and start by building your ship.

[3] Ruskin Bond, *Tales from My Heart*, Red Panda: New Delhi, 2021.

RESILIENCE: WIN IN WEI-JI

'You can never tell just how close you are, it may be near when it seems so far.

So stick to the fight when you're hardest hit, it's when things seem worst you must not quit.

For all the sad words of the tongue or pen, the saddest of these are, "It might have been."'

– John Whittier

WHEN I JOINED MCKINSEY AS A BUSINESS ANALYST, I expected I would be sitting in boardrooms and consulting with senior executives on strategic matters. I was convinced that, dressed in a suit and delivering intense presentations, I would be solving some of the most complex problems of the corporate world – at all of 22.

My first project was a cost-cutting study for an electronics retailer, and two weeks into the job, I was sent to Dallas, Texas. Because it was a cost-cutting project, we had to understand every function of the business in detail, including how employees in the stores spent their time. As a junior analyst, I had to walk around the store with a time sheet and a stopwatch, cataloguing how long people took to perform various functions in the store – unloading the truck, loading the warehouse, putting tags and products on the shelves, selling to a customer and cash management. This started at 5 a.m. with loading at the warehouse and ended at 10 p.m. when cash counters closed. The entire day, I diligently filled in sheets divided into 15-minute intervals, and after the day ended I came back to the hotel and prepared sheets for the next day till well past midnight. This went on for six days a week, including Saturday, Sunday and the Thanksgiving break, because these were the busiest days for retail outlets between September and December.

Three weeks into this, I began to hate my job. Call it a massive collapse of (unrealistic) expectations, the aftermath of working excruciatingly long days or the mundaneness of following people around all day recording their activities – it felt miserable. I had the job that many people dreamt of and there I was sitting in a store bathroom crying, wondering what exactly I was doing with my life. And, of course, I

> **ALMOST ALL JOBS ARE LOWER ON GLAMOUR AND HIGHER ON 'GRUNT WORK' THAN THEY ARE PERCEIVED TO BE. BUT IT IS THE GRUNT WORK THAT TEACHES YOU THE MOST AND TOUGHENS YOU UP.**

couldn't tell my friends and family anything, because, really, no one complains about a job at McKinsey!

Chances are most people have a version of my story from their first few years of work, or even from later into their careers. It's just that no one tells these stories (definitely not during placements in college!) and no one prepares you to live them. Somewhere amid the glamour of big brands, pitching your skills to polished interview boards and all the trappings that come with a corporate career, we forget the reality of a job. Almost all jobs are lower on glamour and higher on 'grunt work' than they are perceived to be. But it is the grunt work that teaches you the most and toughens you up.

My engagement manager (EM), a senior consultant who ran the project, had done the right thing by assigning me the tasks she did – she forced me to do the hard yards. Those time sheets taught me the importance of collecting data precisely and the extended hours made me familiar with the finest details of how stores operate, from price tag labels being placed under different kinds of electronics to warranties upsold during the checkout process. Many of the final recommendations we made to the client were a result of a complete understanding of these finer details. The time we spent on the shop floors also built tremendous trust not just with the senior management team of the client but also the ground teams, making it easier to finally implement our suggestions. 'Consulting isn't frameworks and presentations. How do you have the right to advise anyone on strategy, Radhika, until you actually understand the business?' my EM later told me. She also reminded me that this was just my first project and that things would get better with each one.

They did.

Over the years, I have seen young professionals become frustrated too early in their careers. Forget making attempts at settling on-board, they look to jump ship even before they have explored it thoroughly. Their reasons for quitting are standard. Sometimes it's a so-called 'bad boss', sometimes it's longer work hours than they had bargained for and sometimes it's the inability to deal with the fact that every job has some amount of 'mundane work'. In my parent's generation, it was not uncommon for people to spend a considerable part of their working life, if not the whole of it, in a single job (permanent jobs were actually an attraction). They grew up in an India that was a land of scarcity, where jobs were hard to come by, incomes were tiny and families large. Job security was thus considered to be very important. In a more abundant India, where the range of opportunities is wider, things have changed 180 degrees. Young people are quitting jobs quickly, sometimes in months, and it is not uncommon to come across the résumé of a 35-year-old that records five or six job changes, some stints lasting less than two years. To employers, this is an immediate alarm bell.

One of the finest pieces of career advice I have heard from one of my former senior colleagues is, 'A good career means surviving prolonged periods of hell in one place.' Prolonged. Hell. One place. Nothing could be more true. He was a fast riser in his industry and always told me that some part of his success could be attributed to his being committed to one company for long enough. Over any extended period, organizations will go through ups and downs, and many of your peers will fade – because they will not have the ability to handle crises or the tenacity to endure it. The statement sounds masochistic and no one signs up anticipating that a job will be hell. But remember, hell on earth can only be a prolonged state, not a permanent one. As young Indians, we naturally possess a drive for growth. But while we are aspirational and driven, and it is good to be that way, not every year will give you what you set out to achieve. There will be years of bad compensation cycles, phases in which you hate your boss, or tough patches for your industry or employer. You just have to have the resilience to ride it out.

The markets profession teaches us again and again about volatility. Over the long term, the stock market delivers to an investor about 12 per cent annual returns on average. By all means, this is a very good number. But 12 per cent isn't a consistent year-on-year outcome. The average is a product of both glorious individual years of 30 per cent and 50 per cent returns, and terribly depressing years of -20 per cent and -60 per cent. My first year as the CEO of Edelweiss MF was a golden run – for me, my industry and for the broader group. Markets were booming, our assets were growing quarter on quarter. We crossed the ₹10,000-crore AUM mark pretty quickly, from a base of ₹6,000-crore. The size of my team more than tripled, the media around us got better, and more distributors wanted to hear what we had to say. Personally, things got better for me as well. In August 2018, I spoke at the Mutual Fund Round Table (MFRT), one of the largest mutual fund conferences in the country, and received a standing ovation from a thousand people. In early September 2018, 'The Girl with a Broken Neck' released and quickly went viral. It was as good a time as it could be.

And then came my thirty-fifth birthday. My milestone birthdays have a strange way of coinciding with bad market events. A few days after my birthday that year, the IL&FS crisis exploded and what seemed like isolated news at the onset threw India into a prolonged two-year credit crisis. The world went into a risk-off mode. People's appetite to experiment with younger brands like ours gave way to the need to find comfort in big established names backed by banks and large corporate houses. In the months that followed, our lives changed. Instead of discussing products and business, we suddenly started talking about the risks associated with our brand, something we never had to deal with before. Our products were often performing better than the competition's, our teams were out there doing everything they could, and yet customers and distributors were reluctant to deal with us, because of a market environment that was totally out of our control. When the outside world asks questions, the inside world grows more nervous. I could feel the team's shoulders drooping and I couldn't blame them. Collectively, we felt like the child who worked the hardest and had the highest grades, but didn't get an award because of his or her last name – even though the last name should not matter in a business like mutual funds, which are independently regulated and capitalized.

It is frustrating to not see results when the outcome is determined by a situation you have no power over. To make matters worse, during this phase I received frequent calls from recruiters asking me absurd questions like whether I was looking for a change given the circumstances. I realized that if this was happening to me, my team was facing worse. By early 2019, conducting day-to-day business had become tough. We ran an event called Konnect, where our leadership team travelled to different cities and addressed large groups of distributors. It was our flagship annual property, but for the first time, in mid-2019, we started asking ourselves if we should go ahead with the event. What if people asked us questions that we didn't have answers to in a public forum?

We debated cancelling it and then decided that we would persist. In fact, that year we covered more cities and stepped up the event in terms of scale. As for the rumours, I opened the five-minute segment at the start of each edition of Konnect with the lines, 'Look guys, I know the first thing on your mind is this crisis and all the noise you hear. Let me just clear the air and give you the facts, so we can focus on the presentation after that...' People usually laughed at that, moved on and listened while we presented. Winston Churchill had once said that the only way you really get through hell, is...well...by just getting through it, and that's what we did through 2019 – we kept finding ways to get through it.

At the end of that year, we won the Government of India's prestigious mandate to launch Bharat Bond (that story comes later). This was just the first in a series of positives that carried us into 2020. We finished 2020 with our monthly numbers better than ever before – numbers we'd once only dreamt of – and the air around changed yet again. We had lived through the worst of times, so that we could see the best of times.

A wise individual once told me that while most people run away from chaos, really good leaders actually love it because it brings their courage, their attitude and their chutzpah to the fore. Teams who can survive a storm together can take on the world when

TEAMS WHO CAN SURVIVE A STORM TOGETHER TAKE ON THE WORLD WHEN THE WEATHER CLEARS.

the weather clears. In January 2021, a departing member of our Mumbai sales team wrote a lovely farewell letter to me saying that I had taught him the power of 'Wei-ji', or persisting through crisis. The Chinese word 'Wei-ji' is broken into two parts – 'wei', which means crisis, and 'ji' which means opportunity. 'Winning in Wei-ji' was the title of the presentation I had made to our distributors two years earlier, during the 2019 Konnect. In his letter, my colleague said it was ironic that we were giving a presentation about making the best of a crisis at a time when we were in the depths of one ourselves. Funnily, two years after I used the word 'Wei-ji' repeatedly on stage, I found out that 'Wei-ji' may be a case of mistaken etymology that gained popularity after John F. Kennedy used it in a number of speeches. Whether it exists or not, its popularity is a reminder of just how far a positive tale can travel.

One person I know who is perpetually smiling

is Anu Aga, currently chairman of the Thermax Group. It is an understatement to say that Anu has been to hell and back. A few years after her first child was born, Anu lost her second daughter, and her second son was born with a hole in his heart. In 1982, her husband, Rohinton, suffered a massive heart attack, and Anu spent two years caring for him as well as running the HR team at Thermax. Things began to look up after his recovery and Thermax went public. On the day Anu was returning from the United Kingdom (UK), Rohinton was on his way to meet her when he suffered another heart attack – a fatal one this time. Within a few days of his death, Thermax put Anu in the hot seat as chairman, now of a publicly listed company. Unfortunately, her appointment at Thermax coincided with a downturn in the economy that took the stock from 400 to 36. Then, two other blows struck a year later, when Anu first lost her mother-in-law and then her 25-year-old son in a car crash. After a panel we participated in together, in Pune, I asked Anu how she had handled a lifetime of tragedy being packed into a few years. 'I stopped asking why I was going through this,' she said. 'I asked for a lot of help and I just got through.' From there on, Anu turned around the business. She shed unrelated investments, reconstituted the board and went on a growth spree. She took over a company that had a turnover of ₹600 crore and when she retired in 2004, handing its charge over to her daughter, its turnover had risen to ₹1,300 crore.

Vincent van Gogh is my favourite painter. In my office, you will see displayed a large print of his famous painting *Starry Night*. During his lifetime, Van Gogh neither earned much respect from his family, nor saw much commercial success. Believe it or not, he could only sell one of his paintings while he was alive. But that did not stop him from creating hundreds of paintings, each worth crores of rupees today. His persistence has a lesson for everybody. He said, 'In spite of everything, I shall rise again; I will take up my pencil, which I have forsaken in my great discouragement, and I will go on with my drawing.'

Putting down your pencil is the easy option. We study investor behaviour in market corrections a fair bit in our business, because corrections bring out the worst in most investors. Many of them stop SIPs out of fear, when any study would tell you that they should be topping them up because the most profitable SIP instalments are the ones that happen in deep market corrections. You invest at lower prices and you collect more units that make money when the market comes back; it is a version of investment Wei-ji in action.

A meaningful journey will put you through meaningful difficulties. You will face your version of the drudgery of following people around with time sheets and you will have frustrating situations that you cannot control because the market environment is the way it is. Don't give up and put down the pencil prematurely. Find your mythical Wei-ji and keep drawing.

CHAPTER 3

THE GOLDEN AAA – AMBITION, AWARENESS, ASKING

AMBITION: SHOOT THE MOON

'Ambition beats genius 99 per cent of the time.'

– Jay Leno

'DO THE ZEROES ON YOUR PAY CHEQUE MATTER?'

Priyanka Chopra was asked this question by a journalist after she became the only female actor to be featured in *Forbes*'s Celebrity Top 10 list in 2017.

'Yes, because I work really hard for them. I've worked really hard to be where I am and I deserve to be compensated for it,' she replied.

Priyanka's bio on Twitter at the moment reads, 'Dreamer. Achiever.' Unlike many of her contemporaries who, when asked about it, attribute their success to luck – almost with a sense of disbelief – Priyanka credits hers to having big dreams and working towards those dreams.

It is hard to be ambitious. It is even harder to own one's ambition.

When I became CEO, perhaps because I was almost 15 years younger than my counterparts in other asset management companies and the only woman at the helm of a business in the industry, I was frequently asked, 'Did you ever think you would reach here at this age?' To me it felt like the corporate version of the moment in beauty pageants when the winner displays mock shock and awe, hands on cheeks and mouth agape, as her name is announced. In response, I often felt people wanted me to say, 'Oh, never. I've just been very lucky. I never thought this would happen.'

IT IS HARD TO BE AMBITIOUS. IT IS EVEN HARDER TO OWN ONE'S AMBITION.

Why must this question be asked of anybody? And even if it is asked, it warrants a different answer. I have been ambitious all my life; I have wanted the best for myself and I have put my best foot forward to get it. Unfortunately, most people, especially women, are held back by social conditioning that pushes us to suppress our ambitions, with lines like, '*Jitni chaadar hai, utna paav phailaao.*' Stay within your boundaries; don't push your limits or your luck.

When I was getting married, I happened to wear a light wedding lehenga instead of a heavier bridal outfit, which often weighs many kilos. Nalin walks quite fast and I kept in step with him, taking my *phera*s around the fire quite quickly. After a few *phera*s, the priest stopped me and told me to slow down. '*Dheere chalo*,' he said. '*Thoda sharmao*.' Slow down. Be a little coy. This is the covert training most women receive: walk slowly, stay demure. When I (and I was joined by my parents in this) didn't cry during my *bidaai*, it created a bit of a stir, because, of course, brides are expected to be sad when they leave their parents' home.

In mid-2020, I was on a vacation with friends and spent an evening hanging out with the children in the group. A friend's 12-year-old daughter asked me, 'Hey, I have heard you are really smart. You run a company, right?'

I laughed and told her I did.

She then told me that all the boys in her class call her a nerd. 'But you know what,' she continued, 'I don't care. I want to do really well and be super successful, and that's perfectly fine.'

After she left to go to bed, I felt an incredible sense of pride and optimism thinking about what she had said. Just two days before this incident, a contemporary of mine had told me, 'Radhika, you're too competitive and you take too much pride in being so.' The words addressed to the two of us were distinct, but the story was the same. When I was 12, I used to squirm at being called a nerd, and only learnt over the years to own the arbitrary labels people throw around. Thankfully, this 12-year-old was more evolved.

Only when you set your aspirations high will you push yourself to take the big leaps that can change your life. As a teenager, I used to play a card game called Hearts on the computer. It was a four-player game in which each player's objective is to collect as few 'negative' cards as possible. The negative cards comprised the 13 cards in the hearts suite (each earned one negative point) and the queen of spades (which earned 13 negative points at once). In the normal course of the game, each player attempts to discard as many negative cards as they can, but the game also has a special rule called 'shooting the moon'. A player can 'shoot the moon' by collecting all the negative cards in the game and, if they do so, the other three players get 26 negative

ONLY WHEN YOU SET YOUR ASPIRATIONS HIGH WILL YOU PUSH YOURSELF TO TAKE THE BIG LEAPS THAT CAN CHANGE YOUR LIFE.

points each in the round. The probability of shooting the moon successfully is extremely low, but if you are successful you earn such a massive lead that you are certain to win the game.

Like cards, sometimes life demands that you try to shoot the moon.

I am blessed with a grandmother who was the first to work in her family, one who pushed my mother to study and work despite my father moving countries every three years, and my mother who has been an equal inspiration for me. When I was in the tenth grade, my mother and I decided that I would go abroad for my college education. I had attended middle school in Nigeria in an institution that had an American curriculum, and at the time I was finishing high school at an international school in Rome. The decision was largely a consideration of the fact that settling down in the Indian system in college would be tricky after an international education. Since I was the first in the family to venture on this path, we had very few people to turn to for advice. In 1998, the Internet was limited to patchy dial-up connections, so a few fat books on America's best colleges and

SOMETIMES LIFE DEMANDS THAT YOU TRY TO SHOOT THE MOON.

the college counsellor at school were the primary sources of information. We learnt two things very quickly: one, that education in the US was extremely expensive and, two, that there was no way we could afford anything more than 10 or 20 per cent of it on a government officer's salary.

There were two ways around this problem – that the schools offer me either a merit scholarship based on my academic performance or a need-based grant called 'financial aid' because of my family's inability to pay the full fees. The latter, as the guidebooks told us, was pretty much impossible for international students to avail of and so we quickly filtered our list to arrive at a limited set of colleges that offered merit scholarships. This ruled out all Ivy League colleges, because they don't offer scholarships on principle.

In the summer between tenth and eleventh grade, a dear family friend of ours, Vijay Jain, visited us. Vijay Uncle, as I called him, was one of the few people close to us who lived in the US, and since he was coming to Rome we asked him to bring a bunch of preparation books for the SAT (the admission test for US colleges) and college guidebooks for us. A few days after he arrived, while we were chatting about my applications, Vijay Uncle asked me where I was planning to apply. I told him my list of schools, and he asked me, 'What are your grades in school?' Ever the proud parent, my mother told him I was at the top of my class, and he instantly said, 'Wait, so why are you not applying to a single Ivy League college?'

'They don't offer scholarships and we can't afford the full fees,' I told him.

'They do offer financial aid,' he replied.

Confident about my research and data, I told him, 'That won't happen. It's really rare for international students to get it. No one does.'

'And...what if you do, Radhika?'

He was right. What if I did? Motivated, I went to my counsellor, a kind and practical British man, for help, saying that we should consider applying for financial aid at Ivy League schools.

'The chances of a student getting into an Ivy League college are one in eight,' he said.

'Okay. I know that.'

'Now, if you apply with financial aid, as an *international student*,' he said, saying the last two words slowly and loudly, 'those chances become one in 40. And one in 40 doesn't happen.'

But Vijay Uncle's voice kept ringing in my years. What if it did? What if in one of those eight Ivy League schools I was the one out of 40?

So I applied to all the schools on my list and also to the most competitive programme, a dual-degree in management and technology (M&T) at UPenn, and every other Ivy League school, with a request for financial aid. While I was rejected by quite a few, the game of chances worked out for me – not once, but twice. Both UPenn and Yale University accepted me with generous offers for financial aid. I finally chose UPenn, because the M&T programme gave me the opportunity to study both business and computer science at the same time.

I had made an attempt to shoot the moon and landed an opportunity I would have never imagined. And I knew that it had happened only because my mother and Vijay Uncle had taught me to embrace my ambitions and chase my dreams.

Many years later, when I recounted this story on a television show, a journalist friend wrote a Twitter DM to me, 'My husband was also the kid of an IFS officer. He thought the same thing you did about financial aid being out of reach at his time, and he didn't apply. He watched the show and wants you to tell your mom how awesome it is that you guys dreamt big. He wishes he had.'

The beautiful thing about aspirations is they don't have to be a prisoner of the present or bound by the odds of success.

I am part of an industry in which size (how much money you manage, your AUM) can subconsciously influence how you think of yourself. Data on AUM is public, and league tables ranking AMCs by AUM are published every quarter, with elaborate comments

THE BEAUTIFUL THING ABOUT ASPIRATIONS IS THAT THEY DON'T HAVE TO BE PRISONERS OF THE PRESENT OR BOUND BY THE ODDS OF SUCCESS.

on who has risen and fallen in rank. Larger players dominate media visibility as well as the attention of clients and distribution partners, and it is easy to fall into the trap of classifying yourself as a big, medium or small AMC. In 2018, two years into the business at Edelweiss MF, I went to a big industry conference. As I was helping myself at the lunch buffet, a gentleman came up to me to say hello. After the pleasantries, he looked at me with a concerned face, and said, 'You know, I feel bad for you.'

'Why?' I asked, because I felt pretty fine about myself.

He said, 'You're the CEO of a small AMC. No one must want to meet you.' I maintained a dignified silence, even though I badly wanted to reply. I understood where the comment came from, but it bothered me, and it continued to do so for months on end.

A few months after this conference, in late 2018, the Government of India put out a mandate for the creation of India's first corporate bond Exchange-Traded Fund (ETF). It was a large and first-of-its-kind mandate, originally announced by the finance minister of India at the time, the late Arun Jaitley, in the Union Budget, and MF were invited to apply. Usually, government mandates are the playing field of state-owned or large private asset management companies, and the bond business is one where size attracts size. When we at Edelweiss MF read about the mandate, we were convinced that this was a chance in a million. If we could crack it, we would finally be able to start a bond business and it would also put our assets in a different league. We were a ₹12,000-crore MF then and this opportunity would give us a minimum of ₹10,000 crores of additional AUM. As Deepak Jain told me, 'If we raise even ₹5,000 crore, our league will change; and if we pull off ₹10,000 crore, we will be roaming in another orbit.'

We applied and ended up being one of the five shortlisted bidders. When the shortlist was made public, *Mint* carried a piece expressing surprise at seeing a 'small MF' called Edelweiss MF in the company of four giants. The bidding day in December 2018 was an exceptionally cold and foggy one in Delhi, and we barely made it in time for the final presentation after some terrible luck with delayed flights. A little before we were called upon to present, one of our competitors, surprised to see us in the room, asked one of my colleagues, 'If you guys get this, will you be able to manage it?' (Thankfully, my colleague told me this story after we did the presentation.)

Edelweiss MF ultimately won the mandate, and the bond ETF, later christened Bharat Bond, changed the course of our business. We had envisioned raising ₹10,000 crore, but between December 2019 when the first issue was made public and December 2021, barely two years later, Bharat Bond is a ₹45,000 crore product line. Among all the press coverage Bharat Bond received during its December 2019 launch, my favourite article was the one written by one of India's best financial journalists, Monika Halan, for *Mint*. She wrote, 'The Bharat Bond story is interesting for many reasons beyond finance. It saw a tiny private sector fund house punch way above its weight with an audacious bid and win. Everyone was surprised

> **YOU CAN EARN YOUR SEAT AT THE TABLE, BUT IT STARTS WITH YOU ASPIRING FOR IT.**

that the winner was a fund house not even a tenth the size of the largest fund house that bid.'[1]

So, remember, have the courage to punch above your weight. Everyone tells the small guy that he is incapable of sitting at the table and should be a silent observer at the back of the room. Don't be content with that, and don't resign to it. You can earn your seat at the table, but it starts with you aspiring for it.

The good news is that young India is getting more and more aspirational, and that this aspiration is not limited to south Mumbai or south Delhi. In fact, it is exploding in so-called small towns. I did a podcast with Ranveer Allahbadia, one of India's biggest youth influencers, popularly known as the 'Beer Biceps Guy', where I talked about the power of big aspirations. After the show, I was flooded with messages from young women sharing and celebrating their ambitions. There were girls from smaller cities without the best higher education opportunities who wanted to create social change in their states, there were girls who wanted to lead

---

[1] Monica Halan, 'The deep driving Indian desire for a secure return', *Mint*, 17 December 2019.

breakthroughs in science and make their parents proud, and there were girls who wanted to lead the nation's biggest corporates as CEOs. Ranveer said on that show that he wanted to create 50 global entrepreneurs through his podcast; the comments on the YouTube video of the show are mostly from young women, saying they are sure they will be on that list. These are girls who have big dreams and are willing to do the work to back them. On the show, I mentioned that my father is from Saharanpur, a district in Uttar Pradesh, and later I received a beautiful email titled 'The Girl from Saharanpur' that ended with the lines, 'I used to go around telling people I will be a CEO. There is no stopping me from achieving my ambition now.'

Growing up, I had a poster in my room that said, 'If you aim for the stars, you will get at least halfway there.' The good thing about setting high goals is that even if you miss, you will land in a reasonably good place. I ask every interview candidate I speak to what they want to be five or 10 years later, and 90 per cent of the answers I hear are on the lines of 'I want to manage a team' or 'I want to grow in my career'. Then, once in a while, I meet a candidate from a humble background, who may be starting off in a line role in sales but looks me in the eye and says, 'I want to be a CEO.' And I tell myself, 'You know, this is someone special.'

In a scene in the Hindi movie *Guru*, Gurukant Desai, the lead character in the film, a self-made industrialist played by Abhishek Bachchan, addresses his shareholders and reels them in saying, '*Banna chahte ho Hindustan ke sabse badi* company?' Do you want to be India's biggest company? He achieves that in the movie, and subsequently gets entangled in a lengthy set of courtroom battles. At the end, he is shown coming out of court, and then as a much older version of himself, addressing his shareholders again. This time, with the same old confidence and swagger, court battles notwithstanding, he asks the shareholders with a grin, '*Banna chahte ho duniya ke sabse badi* company?' Do you want to be the world's biggest company? There's something to learn from his chutzpah.

Speaking of audacity, in October 2021, *Mint* wrote an article about how new asset management companies should approach the business. When I congratulated a friend who was going to lead one of the featured new entrants, he told me, 'Go read the article. Tell your team to as well.' I read it and I am glad I did. Three years after that bid in Delhi, and two years after the product launch, *Mint* captured both the success of a so-called 'small' MF winning a large mandate and the impact that the product had on our industry. The lines read, 'Gupta's team pulled

BIG OR SMALL IS A MINDSET, AND HOW YOU CHOOSE TO THINK WILL SHOW IN EVERYTHING YOU DO.

off the unthinkable. Bharat Bond ETFs were born and passive investing had come to debt mutual funds. The launch was followed by a series of copycat products from the rest of the industry. The success threw open the door to product innovation [in mutual funds], a strategy new entrants are banking on now.'[2]

Big or small is a mindset, and how you choose to think will show in everything you do. The world will try to define you and limit you in a set of boxes, and it will send forth probabilities and league tables over which you have no control. As I tell my team, there is only one league table that lives in our heads. It is the one that we define. In that league table, think that you are number one; in that league table, shoot the moon.

2 Neil Borate, 'Meet the upstarts shaking up India's mutual funds sector', *Mint*, 7 October 2021.

AWARENESS: KNOW WHAT YOU DO NOT KNOW

'You are allowed to be both a masterpiece and [a] work in progress, simultaneously.'

– Sophia Bush

LIKE MOST KIDS GROWING UP IN THE NINETIES, MY brother and I watched the *Tom and Jerry* cartoon show regularly on television. Both of us loved Jerry. While Tom was the big cat, constantly on the mouse's trail, Jerry, at a fraction of Tom's size, always found a way out, leaving Tom frustrated and irritated. The mouse knew that what he lacked in size he could make up in agility and intelligence, and he played a smart game – retreating when the time demanded it, charging ahead when he was on stronger footing. Each of us encounters our own moments of being a little Jerry taking on a bigger Tom, but to have a shot at victory we have to start by understanding ourselves. To have a real chance of getting where we want to, we need to understand where we will stumble.

As we grow up, some of our schools put us through self-assessment tests that are supposed to tell us about our strengths and weaknesses, and hopefully shape our choice of further studies and careers. I took a lot of these tests and, unfortunately, didn't pay much attention to what they were saying. I now know I should have. For one, I would then have been aware that my single biggest weakness is 'maps and directions', and perhaps I would not have failed two driving tests or crashed into a car in a client's parking lot on my first day at McKinsey!

I got my first so-called training on answering the 'what are your strengths and weaknesses' questions during campus placements. The standard advice was to prepare a long list of strengths and handle the weakness question with a 'clever' touch. In the case of the latter, try to get away by being funny, by saying something like, 'My weakness is dark chocolate', and then if an interviewer really pushes you, give a strength packaged as a weakness, like, 'I work too

> **TO HAVE A REAL CHANCE OF GETTING WHERE WE WANT TO, WE NEED TO UNDERSTAND WHERE WE WILL STUMBLE.**

hard' or 'I struggle when other people don't work as hard as I do on a team'.

This standard advice, I've learnt, needs to be taken with a spoon of salt.

Scottish writer Thomas Carlyle once wrote, 'The greatest of faults is to be conscious of none.' Packaging or hiding weaknesses may sound practical during campus placements, but your career will demand that you understand your weaknesses and acknowledge them. Of course, admitting that there are things you are not good at, to yourself and then to the world outside, is hard. Yet, the sooner and the more brutally you start doing it, the quicker you can start working on yourself and moving up the pole. I learnt this for the first time in 2016, a few years after Forefront had been acquired by Edelweiss, when I sat down to have a career-related conversation with my boss.

We were building up the hedge fund business (called 'Multi-Strategy Funds') after the acquisition, and I felt settled and connected. But by now I wanted to do more. So he and I sat down in the rather crowded Edelweiss cafeteria (someday I have to ask him why he chose the cafeteria for this conversation and not his office!), and he asked me what I saw myself doing in five, 10 and 20 years.

'Don't tell me. Write it on this piece of paper,' he said. I had been asked this question for the first time, and instinctively I wrote down, 'Run a bank. Run an insurance company. Become CEO of a big financial institution.' He told me that it was great I was this ambitious and wanted to be the CEO of a large retail financial services business, and added, 'Now, on the other side of this paper, write down the skills you think this CEO needs to have and think about which ones you have.'

This 'chit exercise' is scary, because on that tiny piece of paper you clearly see what you want to be and at the same time it becomes starkly apparent how much remains for you to do to get there. Among other things, the first quality I had written down was 'people leadership'. Pretty obvious, because anyone who runs a large institution manages thousands of people. The fact was that until then I had, directly or indirectly, managed a total of six people. The exercise made me realize I still had a lot of work left to do to achieve my goal. I needed greater exposure to working with different kinds of people at various levels of seniority, winning their confidence and trust, and managing them through sticky situations. The question was how was I to make this happen.

A few months after the 'chit chat' with my boss, he called me to his office one day to say that the group MF, one of the younger businesses within Edelweiss and a business he oversaw, was going to acquire the assets of a multinational mutual fund company ('acquiree') almost three times its size. It was a deal that would make big news and would be announced the next day, but it would take six months of integration and extensive regulatory approvals before the business would be ours. He told me he wanted me to run the merger and integration and, at the end of our conversation, added, 'I am not saying much, but if you do well, trust me, this will change you.' I didn't pay much attention to his statement, but I took on the opportunity as a chance to do something new, even though I was confused as to why he was trusting an individual with no experience in the mutual fund industry to run a complex merger.

Well, he was right. The merger did change me, and it changed the course of my career. The deal in question was more than a legal or an operational merger. It involved engaging with employees of two companies with very different cultures and bringing them together as one team. A big part of the success of the final merger was conditional on the acquiree's team joining Edelweiss (this was left to each individual's discretion), and so making the team feel comfortable and building a relationship of trust with them became a core aspect of my job. In these six months, I did things I had never done before, from learning how to speak to edgy people in a public townhall to making sensitive decisions about who would fill specific roles in the organization. I learnt to engage with and drive outcomes for 80 people, none of whom reported to me and over whom I technically had no authority. In doing this and handling people who were in a difficult emotional state because of the uncertainty of the merger and the change in their place of employment, I learnt how to tame my emotions. Difficult conversations are not easy for me to handle and there were days when I struggled to get through them. One night, while driving to Colaba with Nalin, I abruptly started crying, wondering why I was doing all of this. When I told my boss about this the next day, he said, 'Just keep at it, Radhika. Talk about the issues with me, but don't give up.' Over the six months, I had countless emotionally packed one-on-one conversations with employees of both Edelweiss MF and the acquiree, and, at the end of the integration, when more than

75 per cent of the acquiree team chose to join us, I was a combination of exhausted, pleased, relieved and, yes, proud. Four years after the merger, I was talking about those times with Manoj Chaudhary, the current head of HR of the larger group, who at the time had been a part of the Edelweiss MF team. He told me that a merger and integration was one of the best leadership training grounds that anybody could get. 'That's why it was given to me, Manoj,' I said. I was fortunate to have as my boss someone who knew this was a missing piece in my puzzle and found a way for me to discover it.

Many of us may not be as fortunate to have such leaders in our lives, but we can create our own chits, a map for where we want to be in order to track the skills we need to possess or acquire to get there. We can bucket these skills into three categories – skills that we have, skills that we don't have even after trying to build them, and skills that we don't have and have not tried to build. Then we need to leverage the first set, because they are our strengths; ensure we work with people who have the second set because we don't (for instance, my leadership team at Edelweiss MF has very good negotiators, because I am not the best at it); and keep seeking opportunities to build the third.

It's sometimes overwhelming and intimidating to realize that we don't have some of the skills to take on the roles we aspire to, but nothing should stop us from constantly and consciously evolving and upgrading.

Kalpen Parekh took on his first CEO role at IDFC Mutual Fund at 38, and now heads DSP Mutual Fund, one of the largest mutual fund companies in the country. He spent a significant number of years in the industry in sales and marketing, but as CEO he now oversees investments. I have always been curious about how he made the transition because investments is a technical domain that requires a very different skills from sales. Managing investment professionals requires you to speak and understand their language, and also build a connect with them, which is much harder when you don't come from their world.

When I asked Kalpen about this, he told me that well before he took on the role of CEO, he had realized that if he was to do well in this business he would have to master the investing side and also know the fundraising aspect. He wasn't afraid to take classes to gain this knowledge – whether at FLAME University in Pune or investment workshops at Harvard Business School, where he

BEING A LEARNER IS A STATE OF MIND.

also got exposure to global investment professionals. In fact, even today, he continues to take classes to master different areas of money management. At his age and the stage in his career he is at, most people would shy away from being in a classroom with kids half their age, but Kalpen is comfortable being a student.

Being a learner is a state of mind. I also believe that if you are hungry enough you will leverage even the smallest opportunities to learn within the organization you work at, which includes participating in activities beyond day-to-day work projects that most people dismiss as 'that extra work that probably won't do much for me'. Kalpen, for instance, says that four years into the business he had the chance to visit the Asia offices of Prudential, a global asset manager, and joint venture partner of ICICI MF, where he then worked on a month-long project that proved to be transformative for him. He took advantage of the fact that he worked for asset management companies that had global partners, and picked up something from each of them – emotional marketing from Prudential, durability in money management from Sun Life and the knowledge of different asset classes from firms like Natixis.

The world is increasingly becoming an open university – a Twitter account gives you access to the best minds in the world for free – and as you learn more, you also learn how much you don't know. I have had the opportunity to work on three merger-acquisition transactions, all of them high-profile and stressful, with senior members of the Edelweiss Board. Much of what I have learnt about statesmanship, urgent decision-making with limited data and closing a deal, is from watching these individuals in action. Asset management is a complex and multi-dimensional business, and there are times when I have felt insecure about not having in-depth knowledge – at least as much as I want – about some parts of the business.

When I joined as CEO, my background being investments, I didn't have sales and marketing experience, a core element of retail financial services. In the first two years of my stint, I spent nearly all my time with the marketing team and meeting distributors with the sales team. I probably met 1,500 people across cities in small groups in year one itself. In my meetings with the marketing team, I would frequently hear the words 'ATL' and

'BTL' thrown around casually by my colleagues and the ad agencies, and I had no clue what they meant. It took me a year to overcome my hesitation and finally ask Niranjan Avasthi, who heads product and marketing, what it meant, and he explained to me that ATL and BTL stand for 'above the line' (which is ads on billboards and TVs) and 'below the line' (which is print newspaper ads) – the 'line' basically referring to 'at eye-level'. Not rocket science, is it? I had been getting stressed about my limited knowledge of these areas, but I realized that rather than being insecure about what I don't know I should just acknowledge my ignorance and learn about it, and not be afraid of 'asking stupid questions'. So I kept at it, asking incessant questions about sales and marketing, even if it drove the teams a little crazy. A few years later, when someone wrote a sarcastic comment on Twitter, calling me a 'sales and marketing CEO', I took it as a compliment even though the individual was trying to troll me.

In college and through the early years of our careers, we spend a lot of time collecting degrees and brands, but it is just as important to accumulate experiences from a variety of projects, workshops and opportunities that may be a little off the beaten path or not a core part of our day jobs. Eventually, these add to our toolkit. When you look at your résumé, you should hopefully not just find a collection of labels that could belong to anyone else, but a string of experiences that have contributed to shaping you into an individual with unique skills. As valuable as it has been to have UPenn and McKinsey on my résumé, what has shaped me is what I've learnt from the start-up days at Forefront, conducting unique merger transactions, seeing a company through a credit crisis and working on a project with the Government of India. I tell myself I have seen money management in its many colours, in developed and emerging countries, dealing with people who invest billions in multiple currencies and those who invest a few thousand rupees – and there has never been a dull moment. Collecting experiences has kept the business interesting for me.

I read somewhere that self-awareness is the 'recognition of your responsibility to create your own reality'. Ambition is incomplete in itself; it needs awareness to give it direction. It is easy to write on the side of the chit that says 'I want this', it's much

AMBITION IS INCOMPLETE IN ITSELF; IT NEEDS AWARENESS TO GIVE IT DIRECTION.

harder to write on the side that says, 'This is what I need to do to get where I want.'

Our first investor in Forefront was a senior UPenn alumnus, Ramanan Raghavendran, and the first thing he did after he became an investor was to ask for data, or the management information system (MIS), related to our business – revenues, costs, rate of growth and so on. Till then, we had never felt the need to publish such a report and I was irritated because, in my point of view, it felt like a lot of unnecessary work for a small start-up team. When I asked Ramanan why he was making us do it, he said, 'I'm not doing this for me. I'm doing it for you. When you see MIS, you will realize where you are going wrong and you will find ways to fix it. MIS is not for the investor; it's a way to make sure the founder is on the right path.'

Weaknesses, in both the business and in ourselves, cannot be covered up with the 'dark chocolate' kind of answers that may work on campus. They need to be visible, in those self-assessment chits, in that MIS, out there for us to understand and address. Far from hating MIS as I first did, I am now a dedicated fan and consider it a prickly awareness tool that is a reminder of an important mantra: To grow, you have to know.

ASKING: BE YOUR OWN KNIGHT IN SHINING ARMOUR

'He who asks a question remains a fool for five minutes. He who does not ask a question remains a fool forever.'

– Confucius

I HATED MANY THINGS ABOUT THE RIGMAROLE OF finding a job on campus, but nothing gave me as many nightmares as the pre-placement cocktail parties hosted by companies. These parties were usually held in the evening, after a company's HR and management teams had made their formal presentations pitching the company to students. They were intended to be casual social events that gave students a chance to interact with the senior management of a prospective recruiter in a relaxed setting. Nalin absolutely loved these events and never missed them. The free drinks and food at some of the best restaurants in Philadelphia played some role in this enthusiasm, but he always said that they created great opportunities to meet the people who would be interviewing you, express your interest in a company and ask questions in a less intimidating environment. I, on the other hand, dreaded these events. They terrified me. I was (and still am) a shy person. I couldn't muster up the courage to initiate conversations and engage in casual chit-chat with people who would be deciding my future two days later, all while trying to look elegant in high heels, and balancing a drink in one hand and a plate of food in the other. Before these events I would stress myself out agonizing over various things: How do I start a conversation? What if I say something and am met with silence? If I join an existing circle of people who are already conversing, am I not intruding? Isn't it improper to say that I am interested in a job? What will they think of me?

Eventually, I told Nalin, 'I'm wasting their time and I'm going to look stupid.'

'You know, if you don't approach them, someone else will,' he replied.

Despite Nalin's moral support, I usually made up creative excuses to skip these events, and if I attended them I did so with the enthusiasm of a two-year-old being made to swallow medicine for a cough.

Looking back I realize that skipping them was a terrible idea. I was giving up a chance to pitch myself for opportunities I deserved just because I was too scared to raise my hand and too caught up with what people would think of me. Drawing attention to yourself is tough, and it starts right from the time when you are in school, too scared to ask your teacher a question when you don't understand what is going on, because you believe that other kids will think you are not smart. It doesn't get any easier in the workplace, where we hesitate to ask for projects, promotions and raises, because we are constantly worried about how we will be perceived. Will they think I am too pushy? Will they call me over aggressive? Will I be labelled as being difficult?

In 2020, I watched a journalist ask Kareena Kapoor on a television interview if she would go up to a director whose work she liked and tell them she wanted to work with them. She said that in today's day and age, absolutely yes – she would do exactly that. *Isn't not asking the problem?*

Guneet Monga, from the same industry, is not only one of the most eclectic film producers out there today (with films like *Lunchbox, Masaan* and *Pagglait* under her belt) but also one of the youngest in the business. In 2010, when she was just 27, Guneet produced a short film called *Kavi*, which was nominated for an Oscar Award. Showing up on Oscars night is a big deal for anyone in the film business, and most definitely for someone like Guneet, who comes from a very humble background and has worked her way up. Unfortunately, at that time, she couldn't afford the flight tickets to the US. Not one to give up, she started writing emails to various wealthy people she could think of, both in India and abroad, over the next few days. No one wrote back to her. Out of sheer desperation and knowing that she was running out of time, Guneet wrote to the then President of India, Pratibha Patil, stating that she was the pride of India and had been nominated for an Oscar Award, and she needed help. Soon, she got a call from the President's office, and got a chance to screen the film at Rashtrapati Bhavan in Delhi. The President did not attend the screening, but Prithviraj Chavan, who was a senior minister then, did. When the screening was over, Guneet went up to him and asked him for tickets for her crew to attend the Oscars, and after a few calls to Air India and the American Embassy, team *Kavi* was on its way to the ceremony. Guneet turned what looked like a pipe dream into reality only because she said, 'I deserve to be supported. Please help me.'

I have taken much longer than Guneet to realize that my career is my responsibility. While I may have a good support system of family and friends, great bosses and advisors, the onus of seeking opportunities lies on me, and me alone. Each time I don't ask for something that I want and that I likely deserve, I am hurting myself – because, as Nalin had said rightly, if I don't ask, someone else will.

By late 2016, the merger of Edelweiss MF and the MNC mutual fund was almost complete. I had done a reasonably decent job of the project and I knew I had established credibility with both teams. At this time, a discussion had begun about the choice of the CEO of the newly merged entity. Having spent nine months on the merger, I knew that this was a business and team I liked, and leading this kind of business would be a good stepping stone to anything else I wanted to do in the retail financial services sector. I also knew that while I didn't come from a retail background, I had solid experience in asset management and could bring a fresh perspective and passion to the role.

While I didn't say it directly, Nalin knew that I wanted the CEO's role and he told my mom about it. Together, they asked me why I wasn't expressing my interest in the role. *Why wasn't I saying it,* they kept asking me.

'I can't do it,' I said adamantly.

I had convinced myself there was no way I could have these interactions. What would happen to my career if I expressed interest and they said no? There were enough reasons to say no if someone wanted to. I had zero work experience in the mutual fund industry, unlike most CEOs of mutual fund companies I was not a well-known face in the distribution community and I was reasonably young to be leading a business in an industry that is highly regulated, has huge media visibility and where age matters a great deal. Nalin and my mom both said that all of this was inconsequential; that I should focus on what I could bring to the table, not on what I lacked. 'You've worked hard. You are capable. You love the business. If you don't ask, this will go to someone else. If you do, there is a *non-zero* chance it will go to you,' they told me.

Somewhat motivated, I told my boss, while discussing the future of Edelweiss MF after the merger, that if he was looking for a CEO for the business he should consider me because I was interested in the role. What I lacked in experience, I told him, I would make up for with unmatched passion, which few others would bring. This was my 'pride of India' moment. He promised to think it over and get back to me. A few months, and I am sure a lot of deliberation later, I was appointed as the CEO of Edelweiss MF. I got the role because the firm, my boss and the Board trusted me and wanted to take a bet on me – not only because I had shown promise and capability, but also because I had asked for an opportunity at the right time. My asking did count. I know now, that no matter what anyone says, the last step matters. It closes the loop. When you know you want something and are capable of delivering the goods, don't wait for people to read your mind or expect them to know what your aspirations are. Take the initiative and have that conversation.

When I talk to people who are just graduating from college or in the early years of their career, especially women, and they ask me for some parting advice, like a broken record I tell them, 'Ask for opportunities.' I have given this advice to people in their twenties and said this at a session at the State Bank of India with women in their 40s, and they

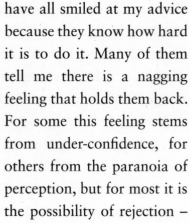

'NO' IS AN OPTION THAT IS ALWAYS THERE ON THE TABLE, AND 'YES' IS A POSSIBILITY THAT IS YOURS FOR THE TAKING. EVEN IF THE ODDS OF IT BEING YES ARE 1 PER CENT, IS IT NOT WORTH ASKING?

have all smiled at my advice because they know how hard it is to do it. Many of them tell me there is a nagging feeling that holds them back. For some this feeling stems from under-confidence, for others from the paranoia of perception, but for most it is the possibility of rejection – what if the answer is 'no'? The way I now think about it is that 'no' is an option that is always there on the table, and 'yes' is a possibility that is yours for the taking. Even if the odds of it being 'yes' are 1 per cent, is it not worth asking?

I have spent a lot of time brooding over the perception battle and what others might think of me if I raise my hand and ask for something. When I had just started my corporate career, a family friend gave me a piece of advice which made sense to me many years later. He said that those who speak up always get more than those who stay silent. There are no points for being shy. Those who ask end up getting the bigger promotions, the raises, the better projects, because they keep vocalizing their needs. When he first told me this I thought it was a slightly cynical view of the world. I have never wanted to be labelled as a 'demanding' person or as being 'too aggressive' or the one who 'always wants more' – and I know this is true of most others. But ever since I started running large teams, I have realized there is a difference between asking and complaining.

Those who ask are genuinely aspirational. They work hard to achieve their ambitions and, at the right time, are not afraid to say, 'I want to try this, and I think I can do it.' They seek to grow, but they do not put others down as they move ahead. Complainers, on the other hand, are a perennially unhappy lot. They constantly compare themselves to other people and want what others have. They also express their unhappiness again and again (and again), which can get grating very quickly.

Four years into the business, a member of my team came up to me, just as I had done with my boss many years ago, and told me that in seven to eight years he aspires to be the CEO of a mid-sized mutual fund company. He told me there were gaps in his profile and that he was looking to develop certain new skill sets. He wanted to take on an additional responsibility that had the possibility of opening up in the near future and asked if he could be considered for it. He was right. An opportunity was going to open up, and while I had never seen him in that role and had planned to hire for the position externally, the conversation set me thinking 'Why not him?' Eventually, he landed the role.

The workplace is a competitive space, but I believe that all of us have a shot at opportunities bigger than we can imagine if we choose not to be held back by artificial fears and limitations. My talk, 'The Girl with a Broken Neck', was a result of my asking for an opportunity. In 2017, I met Captain Raghu Ramanan, as a part of a weekend workshop on storytelling, and while I am usually suspicious about training programmes, this one spoke to me in a way no session had until then. On the second day of the programme, after a session of theoretical training, Captain Raghu asked each of us to deliver a 15-minute TED-style talk and share a personal story. At the end of the day, when I was leaving the workshop, he told me to stay in touch with him and added, 'Radhika, you will go really far. You have a lot of potential.'

A few weeks after the training, Captain Raghu sent us an email saying that TEDx had a few open slots around the country and asked if any of us would like to try formally speaking on this platform.

Maybe it was his last comment from the workshop that had stayed with me, but I called him the next day and said, 'Captain, do you think I can try this? I am not sure I am ready, but can I try?' Captain Raghu responded to my question with enthusiasm and commitment, and said he would coach me through the process. A couple of months later, I was on stage, speaking at TEDx TISS. While that talk never released, my second attempt 10 months later, 'The Girl with a Broken Neck', did come about, and it went viral.

My storytelling journey thus started with me putting my hand up for an opportunity and now I consider myself to be truly bitten by the storytelling and public-speaking bug!

Every instance of putting one's hand up may not have this outcome, of course. There are real 'no's, and they sure pinch. I had once called a mentor to ask him about an opening that I thought I was a fit for, and he told me, very candidly, that I was overreaching and should build up my skill set a little more before attempting it. 'You just need more experience to do this right, Radhika. Now isn't the time.' I felt pretty bad hearing this and sulked for a few days. But I've learnt since then that occasional rejection should not stop you from asking again, maybe after doing a little more homework or preparing yourself better.

At UPenn, as you move into your third and fourth year, class participation becomes an important part of your academic performance especially in business classes. In my fourth year, I took a class on Business and Public Policy, where participants were awarded points each time they raised their hands to ask a question. It was an intimidating experience for students usually too hesitant to be heard even when they had a genuine question, but since our grades depended on it we all took to it quickly. In a way those finance classes mirror the workplace – you get points for raising your hand. While the probability of getting what we want is hard to predict and may be low, the potential upside of asking is usually very high and the potential downside much lower than we estimate. Any finance person would say that's a good trade.

So go out there and ask for what you think you deserve. As Tata Sky puts it in one of my favourite ads, '*Poochne mein kya jaata hai? Kabhi pooch daala, toh life jhingalala.*'

CHAPTER 4

FRESH AIR AND UNACCU- STOMED EARTH

CHANGE: CATCH THE CYCLE EARLY

'You cannot swim for new horizons until you have courage to lose sight of the shore.'

– William Faulkner

RETIREMENT DAY IS A BIG EVENT IN THE LIFE OF A government officer. From the time you join the service in your 20s, you know that this day will eventually come. However, unlike the corporate world, where retirement brings a 'finally I'll be free' vibe, for those who serve in the government it is often accompanied by a sense of melancholy and even fear. Government officers command both power and perks but lose many of these privileges after retirement. The attitude of people towards them changes, and often the network of friends and the extended family shrinks as well.

Retirement week can never be easy, but my father's was particularly so and rather unique. Knowing his story might help you understand why.

My father's journey is the very definition of the 'Indian dream'. Born in Gangoh, a small town in Saharanpur district in Uttar Pradesh, he grew up in a household of modest means in Delhi, studied in a Hindi-medium school and bided his time as a lecturer at Rajasthan University for a couple of years so he could afford to pay the fees for the Indian Administrative Services (IAS) coaching classes he had enrolled in at Rau's IAS Study Circle. He finally cracked the prestigious Indian Foreign Service, ranking seventh, and from 1976 to 2010 he had a glittering career representing a changing India abroad, serving in Brazil, Pakistan, US, Italy, Zambia and, finally, Denmark, from where he retired as Ambassador.

Across these intercontinental moves, my mother stood by him, working as a kindergarten teacher, having given up a potentially sparkling corporate career after graduating from St. Stephen's College, New Delhi. She changed jobs with each of his postings, took on the duties of hosting diplomatic parties, mastered the art of making samosas at scale and decorating our entire home in orange, white and green on India's Independence Day and Republic Day. My parents have a 10-year age gap between them. They had a love marriage, unconventional for their era, and have remained partners in crime through their time together.

My father's last week at work was full of celebrations. It was a special week, ahead of the change that loomed. His fellow Ambassadors from different nations were hosting parties for him, the Queen of Denmark had planned a formal farewell and he was hosting a final event during which he would make his last address as a representative of India. That week, my mother was not with him. For his closing party, his final speech and his last move back to India, he was alone. He wanted it this way. A few months before he retired, my mother had flown down to Delhi, where they would ultimately live, to look for a home and her next teaching opportunity. My father was due to retire in August 2010, by which time school years are already in session in India, and she needed to have her job in place in advance. In June that year, a prestigious school in Gurgaon offered her a role as the principal of the primary school. But there was a catch: She would have to join in July, before the school year started, and that meant she would have to leave my father alone in Denmark. My mother says it took them less than five minutes to decide. 'You followed me around the world for so many years, but now the future is about your career and your job. That comes first,' he told her. He knew his career, however glorious, was coming to an end, but my mother, who was ten years younger, still had many years of teaching ahead of her.

My father chose the future over the past, something he has always done. The government ranks every country on a scale from 'A' to 'C' (A being the easier countries to live in and C being the difficult ones) and, in the spirit of fairness, A postings are usually followed by C postings, and vice versa. For my brother and I, these moves weren't always easy – they meant leaving behind a home, school and friends we'd grown to love. But my parents approached each new change with a sense of optimism. My father taught us to look forward to what lay ahead, rather than cry over what had been and, contrary to our fears, he handled his retirement in the same way. He built a home in Gurgaon and today he runs the house with as much gusto as he ran his embassy. He reads voraciously, writes for a number of publications, and shares his views on various news channels about international affairs. As he puts it, he is the busiest among all of us and has never been happier with his life.

CHANGE IS A REALITY, AND MOVING FORWARD IS A NECESSITY.

During my work on Bharat Bond at Edelweiss MF, I made a number of trips to the Ministry of Finance, which is in the North Block of the Rashtrapati Bhavan, right opposite my father's former office, the Ministry of External Affairs. When I talk to him about visiting South Block, where the Ministry's offices are located, he reminds me that while he cherishes every second of the time he spent there, his life today is his current office at home, overlooking the garden. '*Woh*,' he says referring to his pre-retirement career, '*ek aur daur tha, guzar gaya. Yeh ek aur daur hai.*' That – the South Block office – was a different era, and that has passed. This is another era.

His attitude holds in it a valuable lesson to learn. We cannot cling to the past. Change is a reality, and moving forward is a necessity. Whether it is a change in your location, a change in organization or a role within the same organization, or even a change in your circumstances or environment, the inescapable fact is that change is inevitable. At times, change is the result of conscious actions on our part, and at times it is forced on us by altered life situations and the passage of time. Whatever the cause, when circumstances change, we must actively make a choice between embracing the future or living in the rose-tinted past of the *purana daur*. Of course, the past is appealing. In a piece for the *Wall Street Journal*[1], scholar Johan Norberg talks about the power of nostalgia, the reason we all long for the 'good old days'. He suggests that holding on to the past gives us a sense of predictability as individuals, and, when done collectively, it becomes a source of communal strength. This phenomenon is so powerful that brands now leverage it. There is a reason Paper Boat packages its thandai and kala khatta flavoured juices as recreations of our childhood favourites, and Cred uses superstars from the 1990s like Jackie Shroff and Govinda to appeal to a credit card user base that grew up in that era. What we forget, however, is that the past was not free of problems. The same problems we grapple with today existed back then – class and communal tensions, how we perceive the people in power, the divide between older and younger generations. It applies in every context of life, as

[1] Johan Norberg, 'Why we can't stop longing for the good old days', *Wall Street Journal*, 26 December 2020.

lyricist Javed Akhtar quipped at the Jashn-e-Rekhta Urdu festival in 2017, 'Why does every man, when he gets married, tell his wife, you make good dal, but not quite as good as what my mother made? Has the quality of dal in India just deteriorated over 1,000 years?' It hasn't! We need to accept today's dal – one slightly different from the one we grew up with – as our reality and move forward.

> **A GUARANTEED WAY TO FAIL IS TO FOCUS ON THE PROBLEMS IN YOUR CURRENT ENVIRONMENT AND COMPARE THEM TO THE POSITIVES OF THE PAST.**

In my induction session for new employees at Edelweiss MF, the first thing I tell them is that if they want to have a chance at succeeding in this organization they have to embrace it and let go of where they came from. They are certain to find problems here, but chances are there was no shortage of problems at their previous organization and if they were to take an honest count there is no shortage of problems anywhere. A guaranteed way to fail is to focus on the problems in your current environment and compare them to the positives of the past.

I have also found that when we seek advice about making a change, what we hear in response can exaggerate our fears. In 2013, after five years of running Forefront and taking it to a certain size, Anant, Nalin and I decided we wanted a larger platform to grow on, one that gave us the advantages of capital and a distribution system. We decided to sell the business.

Selling a business in financial services is a little different from selling a tech or a consumer company. In money management, the buyer perceives a significant amount of value in the founding team, and they usually have to continue as employees for a certain period after the sale. A sale then is not just a sale, but a decision about where to spend the next four or five years of your career. As we started working with our investment banker on the deal and meeting with prospective buyers, we turned to people around us for advice. About 80 per cent of those we spoke to said selling the company was a terrible idea. Ironically, when we had made the move to India to set up Forefront here, about 80 per cent of our advisers had told us the same thing – that it was a terrible idea. 'Why do you want to give this up and work for someone else? Indian companies are *lala* companies, they can never be run professionally.' As young professionals who had never worked in India earlier, hearing this left us spooked. Similarly, during the selling of Forefront to Edelweiss, we were told, 'They will eat you alive. They are so aggressive.' To this day we laugh at the fact that we began by being hesitant to even meet Edelweiss, the place we finally ended up at, because of the fear planted in our minds.

Change is a two-sided coin but, at the time, the world around us seemed to be focused only on the negatives of selling the company and the positives of running it ourselves. At some point, I told Nalin that we needed to stop discussing what was great at Forefront and start thinking about what we could create at Edelweiss. We sold the company on 30 April 2014 and I was more emotional that day than I would have imagined. I remember taking the Forefront sign off the door of our Worli office and carrying it to the car as we packed up. Then we crossed the Bandra–Worli Sea Link to the Edelweiss office in Kalina. We had done the Worli–Kalina trip countless times over the previous months while I had led the negotiations for the deal, but I cried as we crossed the bridge that day. All the things we'd been told by people around us came rushing into my head, the foremost being that our status would change from that of owners to employees. We had planned on going straight to our desks when we

reached Edelweiss House, but we were told that
Rashesh wanted to meet us. I don't remember
what happened in that meeting, but I know I felt
much better after it. There was a surprise party to
celebrate the deal that night and by the time Nalin
and I returned home we were both smiling, excited
about what was to come. The future, it turned out,
was not as bad as people had made it out to be.
In the deal, it had been decided that we'd have to
work for Edelweiss for four years, and as I write
this, I have been here for many more years than
that. Now, every time someone asks me for advice
about selling a company, I tell them to think about
it with an open mind and not focus on the negatives.
I also ask them to remember that we were not eaten
alive; rather, the sale and change created a whole
new set of opportunities for us. As for the change
of status from owner to employee, I will only say
that entrepreneurship is a state of mind, not a state
of employment!

One thing that keeps me going in the investment
profession is that it is so dynamic. Economies and
stock markets have different cycles and there is no
one investment approach that always works. There
will be times when new-age fast-growing companies
will outperform traditional stable businesses, and

then the environment will quickly reverse; there will be times when larger companies are in favour over smaller ones, and then the trend will change. A cycle can last a few years, sometimes even five to eight, or even a decade, but very few investors are able to understand early enough when a cycle will change; they are unable to 'catch' the cycle at the right time, so to say, and place their bets. The few that have the ability to do this end up making disproportionate returns.

We lived my childhood in three-year cycles thanks to my father's postings, but because my parents taught us to move forward quickly we learnt to enjoy them from day one. If they had resisted change, we perhaps would never have made the most of the unique experiences each of the countries we lived in had to offer us in the short time that we had.

In a book of stories chronicling the lives of Indians living through change titled *Unaccustomed Earth,* one of my favourite authors, Jhumpa Lahiri, quoted these words from British writer Nathaniel Hawthorne: 'Human nature will not flourish, any more than a potato, if it be planted and replanted, for too long a series of generations, in the same worn-out soil. My children have had other birthplaces, and, so far as their fortunes may be within my control, shall strike their roots into unaccustomed earth.'

All of us seek growth – in our country, in our economy, in our careers and in our lives – but growth is predicated by change, both internal and external. If we don't want to stagnate, we will have to find within us the ability to constantly relish the smell of new soil and tread with confidence on unaccustomed earth.

ADAPTABILITY: LEARN TO PIVOT

'It's no use going back to yesterday, because I was a different person then.'

– *Alice in Wonderland*

THE KAKAPO IS A WEIRD BIRD. IT LOOKS LIKE AN OWL, walks like a duck and has the posture of a parrot. Classified as one of the largest birds on Earth, the creature weighs up to 4 kilograms and, for a long time, thrived in New Zealand, which provided a comfortable habitat for it. Despite being a flightless bird, the kakapo lived a pretty happy existence. Its biggest threat was defending itself from the eagles on the islands it inhabited and evolution aided it greatly in this, bestowing it with emerald-green feathers that helped it blend into the surrounding foliage. But then, 800 years ago, humans started showing up on the islands. They brought boats and other mammals, including rats, cats and sheep, forever changing the face of what had been known as the 'land of birds'. This weird-looking bird, which had thrived so far by evolving its defence strategies against eagles and other birds, was suddenly rendered powerless when its environment changed. The kakapo is now virtually extinct. There are only 200-odd adult kakapos alive today, in four islands off the New Zealand coast.

As students, most of us will remember being taught Charles Darwin's conclusion that the most important factor for survival is neither size, nor intelligence, nor strength. It is adaptability.

Being adaptable sounds like an easy thing to do, but in practice it can be quite challenging. My mother learnt this in both hard and humorous ways as a woman trying to bring up two small children in constantly changing environments across countries and continents. We lived in Delhi from 1991 to 1995, and that was an easy environment for her. Delhi is the city of her birth, both sets of my grandparents lived there, we went to one of the better schools and lived in a government colony on Tilak Marg in central Delhi. Then, in 1995, when I was 12, my father was posted to Lagos, Nigeria, and life there was anything but comfortable. All the little things that most of us take for granted became impossible to avail of there – from not being able to buy fresh milk and switching to milk powder, to not having access to basic shops and malls that sold affordable clothes, and living in a cash-driven economy where law and order was so challenging that homes came with bulletproof doors and windows. Robberies were routine and almost every household had its own story of one or the other family member being held at knife or gunpoint. Through all this, my mother simply refused to give up. Ready-made clothes were not available, but she found ways to design clothes and get them made. So she would drag me to Yaba, the local cloth market in Lagos, and buy rolls of cotton, silk and denim. Then she would find a local tailor and put her design skills to work. Most of the dresses I wore at the time were thus inspired by Bollywood movies which she watched keenly, pausing the VCR when dance sequences came on to copy the costumes worn by Karisma Kapoor in *Dil Toh Pagal Hai* or *Hero No. 1*, or for that matter any of the other female lead actors. All the clothes were embellished with fake designer labels that the tailor insisted on stitching on – 'Nikke' instead of Nike, or 'Guccci' instead of Gucci. Our family's collective pastime, the game of Bridge which helped me land the job at

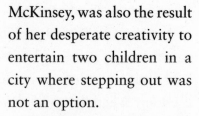

ADAPTABILITY STARTS BY OWNING YOUR NEW SURROUNDINGS AND DOING SO WITH A GENEROUS DOSE OF OPTIMISM AND HUMILITY.

McKinsey, was also the result of her desperate creativity to entertain two children in a city where stepping out was not an option.

In 1998, my father was posted to Italy and all these challenges evaporated, especially the problem of finding clothes, as we moved to one of the most fashionable countries in the world. My mother quickly abandoned designing and took to scouting for shoes in the open markets of Rome. She also insisted that we use the opportunity to travel all over Europe, no matter how restricted our budgets were, even if it meant eating aloo-puri on the Alps. In the three years that we lived in Nigeria, we were unable to travel. I was 15 when we moved to Italy and this was the last time we would be together as a family before I left for college. 'Let's make the most of it,' she would tell us, no matter the situation. A high adaptability quotient is a sought-after skill in corporates today, but my mother, like most Indian mothers, always had bucketloads of it.

Adaptability starts by owning your new surroundings and doing so with a generous dose of optimism and humility. When we join a new role, we often come to it believing that 'everything is broken and I am here to fix it'. Most of us are convinced that we have some magical skill that nobody else possesses and that because we have had success in the past we can suddenly turn everything around in the present as well. Success, however, does not always export well. The skills that make us successful in one environment do not necessarily carry over to the next; there is a reason the class topper is not often the most successful entrepreneur or corporate professional. I have been guilty of believing I am Ms Fix-It, and I have ended up articulating it unconsciously by saying things like 'let's clean this up' or 'let's repair this', until a colleague at Edelweiss MF asked me to reflect on how these words would make the existing team – who had been there all along – feel. Why not rephrase the problem and tell yourself and others around you that you joined a situation where things are good, but want to focus on making them better? It is definitely more energizing to improve a working ship, than to repair a broken one!

A lot of us make the mistake the kakapo made – underestimating our new environment and the competition around us. When Nalin and I moved back from the US to India to start Forefront, in the very first week, my father-in-law asked us to visit a few of his friends, who had retired after working in financial services in India, to get advice on starting a business (and I think to drill some sense into our young US-returned heads!). One of my most memorable meetings was with a family friend, a former head of HDFC Securities, whose no-nonsense attitude belied his gentle disposition. Over many bowls of bhelpuri in his Goregaon home, the three of us told him that we had returned to India to start a portfolio management services (PMS) business and were confident it would scale up quickly. He told us that two prominent global brands – Franklin Templeton and DSP Merrill Lynch – had recently shut down their PMS businesses in India. We protested at once, 'But we have Wharton degrees, and we are going to be a boutique business. Our approach will be different.' He patiently heard us out and agreed that there was every chance that we would do well. But he also told us one thing I haven't forgotten. Many people who move from the US to India have a sense of superiority about what they bring to the table and what they can achieve in the country. They whine about the traffic and inefficiencies, oblivious of the fact that they have to work with the existing infrastructure. They forget that they will compete with people who live in India, who have built meaningful businesses and experienced grand success. This success has come to them because they have real skills that are locally relevant and not just because of dumb luck. 'You are so charmed by your global pedigree and work experience that you don't even understand the threats and competition around you,' he told us. 'If you don't accept India wholly and truly, you are setting yourself up for failure.'

In every transition I have made since then, I have tried to remember his advice. I have understood that when you accept your environment, you will also accept feedback and act on it quickly. A UPenn classmate of mine, Kunal Bahl, co-founder of e-commerce giant Snapdeal, is a case study in building a business by adapting and pivoting, based on feedback.

Kunal's first business in early 2008 was actually an online movie ticket-booking business, before platforms like BookMyShow existed. Soon after he started, he and his co-founder realized that they lacked the experience of building an Internet business and cinema chains came back to them with the feedback that the economics of the business they had envisioned wouldn't work. At this time, there was both a lot of buzz about and investment in retail in India, and so they made their first pivot: selling coupon books to retail outlets, who would give deals to customers. Within a short span of time, by sheer brute force and hard work, they had signed up 150 retailers and restaurants. Unfortunately, within three months, they realized that retail distribution was hard to build and harder to make money on, and that in the process of building the business they were simply accumulating a lot of perishable coupon booklet inventory. At the same time, in early 2008, mobiles were starting to become more common in the country. Could they take away the challenges of the physical coupon booklet and move offline sales to mobile, they asked themselves. So they pivoted yet again to selling scratch cards on the mobile, essentially a product that enabled a consumer to receive coupons on their mobiles when they were near an outlet, and within a few months they acquired 2,00,000 users. Unfortunately, these were 'freemium' or unwilling-to-pay-customers, and when they were asked to pay up, only 1,000 of them stayed on. Kunal and his partner then pivoted to selling coupon cards valid for 12 months (not perishable) to corporates in a business model that blended offline and online.

While all this was happening, merchants they had worked with over the previous year and a half started pushing them to distribute their coupons through an online site, an Indian analogue to Groupon, which was a global rage at the time. Till this point, technically, no business had worked for them, but they had built valuable relationships with merchants who were giving them feedback. And so they made their fourth change in one and a half years, testing the online business without shutting down their offline business, launching what became Snapdeal, with one designer and one developer as staff. When they began, their goal was to reach 100 transactions a day in three months; they got there in three weeks. The deals space became competitive and they quickly recognized the need to pivot from a deal a day to a wider assortment of deals, something no other market player did. By June 2011, in large part because they had the foresight to adapt, they had captured 70 per cent of the deals market. As Kunal puts it, after facing extreme and repeated failure despite putting in so much hard work when you see the needle move the way it did with Snapdeal you give it everything you can. Despite their deals business booming, when customers began writing in saying they'd like to buy physical products on the website, the founders listened. Selling products online was a whole new ballgame, but bit by bit they built it up to sell physical products.

This was a time when venture capitalists were also talking about the scale of Internet businesses in China, so Kunal went to China to understand that business. He says that trip was valuable because as a market the country was four to five years ahead of India; it was also easier to relate to, compared to the US, which was 10 to 12 years ahead. The China trip reconfirmed the potential size of the e-commerce opportunity in India, and the team quickly ramped up to tackle it head on. This was the foundation of Snapdeal 1.0, a multi-product e-commerce company.

I have known Kunal since his coupon card days. He is hardworking and extraordinarily sharp, but what distinguishes him from others who have big dreams is that he is a master of the pivot – evident in the seven big moves he made in three years! Kunal isn't disheartened by failure but learns from it. He collects feedback and shifts gears quickly, often without having all the answers in place, and he channels his creativity to find the opportunity in the problem. Of course, his adaptability story doesn't end there – there's still the Snapdeal 2.0

story to come. But that is for
another day!

> **ADMITTING THAT YOU DON'T HAVE ALL THE ANSWERS IS OFTEN THE FIRST STEP TOWARDS FINDING THEM.**

In taking on new roles, I have also found that sometimes, in the workplace, curbing your enthusiasm to contribute and just stepping back and being a learner helps. When you are humble and open to asking questions, people go out of the way to not just teach you but help you succeed. Admitting that you don't have all the answers is often the first step towards finding them.

When I joined as CEO, I was raw on many fronts, new to managing a large team (many of whom were older than me), new to the dynamics of the mutual funds industry, and new to many functions. I knew little about sales, as also marketing, public relations (PR), operations and much more. Yet, I carried the title of CEO, leading a business that had just seen the merger of two firms. Thankfully, my boss at the time had run many businesses of which he did not necessarily have the history or background when he started, and he had managed people older than himself. One piece of valuable advice he gave me when I started was to free myself from the pressure to add value. He told me that a fancy title makes you want to go into a meeting and contribute immediately – to speak, to suggest an improvement, even if you have no idea what is happening in the meeting. It is a way to justify your role. 'Don't fall for this,' he said. 'Go into meetings and, for a few months, just listen quietly. Then start asking questions if you don't understand something. Take the time to find your feet.'

His advice really helped. When I realized I didn't need to add value, I just asked questions about what I didn't understand and people were very patient about answering them. My colleagues in sales uncomplainingly explained how to price SIPs and how to interpret the data that was released in the mutual fund world. The compliance team performed multiple walkthroughs with me on how MF regulations are distinct from other money management industries that I was familiar with and didn't mind me asking the same questions again and again. In July 2020, the marketing team sent me a document on a search engine optimization (SEO) review, and while I know the basics of SEO, when I opened the document I found that some of the slides were Greek to me. I called Manisha Dokania, the head of marketing, and asked if she could do a one-on-one session with me so I could understand the words and numbers, and she did so happily.

YOUR LEARNABILITY IS YOUR SUPERPOWER.

One of my French teachers when I was a teenager in Lagos had once told me that if you think you are a lone soldier who has to just trudge along, you have already lost the battle. As Professor Dumbledore told Harry in J.K. Rowling's *Harry Potter and the Deathly Hallows*, 'Help will always be given at Hogwarts to those who ask for it.'

Martial arts genius Bruce Lee had once quipped, 'The greatest fighter is not a boxer, karate or judo man. The best fighter is the man who can adapt to any style. He kicks too good for a boxer, throws too good for a karate man and punches too good for a judo man.' In today's world, each of us will likely hold many different jobs across our careers, and maybe even have three or four different careers, some of which we can't fathom at the age of 22. In such a world your learnability will be your superpower. Know not just how to box, how to kick, and how to throw, but also when to employ each of these techniques. The most powerful game you can play is to keep learning to play new games in new ways.

COMPARISONS: DON'T HUG THE BENCHMARK

'Comparison is the thief of joy.'

– Theodore Roosevelt

WE ALL KNOW A 'SHARMA-JI *KA BETA*'. YOU CAN replace Sharma with Shah or Srinivasan or Sengupta, depending on which part of the country you live in, or replace '*beta*' with '*beti*', and you will find that this particular character remains oddly familiar. Sharma-ji *ka beta* is that kid in our neighbourhood who tops his class, gets into a great college, then finds himself a job at a reputed MNC, and finally marries a girl duly approved by his parents and in a few years produces two kids who are just as perfect as him. He is the pride of his parents and the envy of everyone else's, and the bane of his peers' existence. He is the yardstick we are constantly compared to, and whatever we do we can never measure up to him.

While we resent this particular monster being in our lives, as we grow up we tend to create our own versions of Sharma-ji *ka beta*, against whom we benchmark our careers and lives. If you asked anyone in my graduating class what they wanted to do in life just six months after they'd started college and hadn't yet attended a single introductory finance class, the response unhesitatingly would be investment banking. Everyone wanted to be an investment banker simply because everyone else wanted to be an investment banker. It's a different matter that two years after graduation most people who had joined investment banking quit because they couldn't handle the pressure of 18-hour days and didn't find the day-to-day work meaningful.

The pressure to conform was so strong that when a lone guy chose to work at Microsoft or a close friend chose to join Google (this was post the dotcom crash in the early 2000s, when tech wasn't glamorous any more), we rolled our eyes and wondered what they were thinking. (Incidentally, one particular Microsoft guy ended up founding a unicorn in India and a Google girl ended up doing pretty well after getting a lot of stock options in 2004.)

I have always been a competitive person and have struggled with the comparison bug. When I graduated from college, all my classmates worked for Wall Street or consulting brands, some bigger and some smaller, but we felt like equals. Ultimately we were analysts living in the same kind of apartments, taking the New York subway to work and eating at the same places on the weekends. Many of my classmates came from business families, but in the circumstances no one's net worth stood out over another's. When we moved back to India, this changed. Nalin and I went from working at powerhouses like Goldman Sachs and McKinsey to being fledging start-up founders, with an office in an industrial estate in Worli that had broken elevators, exposed wiring and stray dogs roaming the corridors. Like many founders, we chose not to take salaries for a few years, and later when we did we allocated ₹50,000 a month for ourselves. We lived in a tiny one-bedroom apartment, and couldn't afford a car until two years after setting up Forefront.

This phase drove me crazy. Friends from college, the same people who felt like equals in New York, now ran large family businesses or worked for big brands, and when they invited us over for dinner their lavish lifestyle and homes made me wonder what I was doing with my life. If we chose to meet friends outside for dinner, I was conscious of our Maruti Swift parked next to their bigger, swankier cars. After each meeting, I would start yet another discussion with Nalin (who never seemed to agree with me) about why we had given up everything for a lifestyle that was so 'inferior' to that of our classmates. These insecurities were completely mine; no one ever said anything to me. In fact, everyone was friendly and gracious, but my Sharma-ji-*ka-beta* syndrome would not stop popping up.

In fact, I could not stop comparing my journey to my friends', even if they became entrepreneurs like us. A couple of years after we returned to India, we started meeting Kunal more often. He was seeing serious momentum with Snapdeal then. We were just getting Forefront off the ground and Kunal, the same age as us, was the talk of the town, especially at UPenn alumni dinners. His photos were splashed all over the newspapers, with him winning award after award, rubbing shoulders with people like Masayoshi Son of Softbank. I had one more person now to compare myself to and another reason to feel unhappy. I would tell Nalin, 'We are fighting to raise a few crores. Look at Kunal's valuations. He went to school with us.' All of Nalin's logical arguments – how our journeys were different, how finance was a different business from e-commerce – failed before the power of my comparisons. My insecurities weren't limited to my peers in India. When my mother, out of harmless curiosity, asked what my salary had been in the US, I cleverly avoided her question, at the back of my mind comparing myself to classmates who were working there. So consumed was I by comparisons that after moving back in 2009 I didn't go back to the US for many years, just so that I wouldn't encounter my friends and acquaintances who had stayed on in big firms and begin to once again question my decision.

All of us have carried this baggage at some point, and for me shedding it has been incredibly hard but very helpful. In his essay 'The Happy Man', Bertrand Russel writes, 'Envy consists in seeing things never in themselves, but only in their relations. If you desire glory, you may envy Napoleon, but Napoleon envied Caesar, Caesar envied Alexander, and Alexander, I dare say, envied Hercules, who never existed.'

Comparisons are both unhealthy and unending.

There will always be someone ahead of you, just as there will be many behind you – depending on *your* definition of 'ahead' or 'behind'. When you think consciously about it, though,

IN CONSTANTLY TRACKING WHO IS 'AHEAD' AND BY HOW MUCH, YOUR FOCUS SHIFTS FROM THE MOST IMPORTANT RACE – YOUR OWN.

you will see that your focus remains sharply on the former. In constantly tracking who is 'ahead' and by how much, your focus shifts away from the most important race – your own. Setting up Forefront was a bold and disruptive long-term move, although in the short term I constantly felt I was 'behind the pack'. If you ask me, I would do it again, and all over again, if I had to.

In money management, if you have to achieve real alpha, that is, deliver significantly higher returns than your peers and the basic market benchmark, you can never do it by simply copying the benchmark. You have to deviate from it, make distinct choices and place your bets. And, to create alpha and wealth in the long term, you also have to live with so-called underperformance in the short term.

When you are obsessed with the benchmark, you can start believing that the world is out to give you much less than you deserve. Never am I as frustrated in appraisal discussions as when I encounter people asking for more compensation or a promotion simply because they are earning less than their batchmate who joined the firm at the same time, or their peer in another organization. Asking for more is always good and encouraged, but you should do it because you deserve it and not for any other reason. Two individuals who graduated together or joined a company together may have a common starting point, but will eventually see very different journeys in their careers that are a function of their performance, choices and background.

I, for instance, graduated in 2005, in the middle of an economic boom in the US, when jobs and visas were easy to find. But many of my friends who graduated three years later, in 2008, after the financial crisis, struggled to find jobs and had to return to India. Our journeys were very different, at least in the short term. The job market may have temporary dislocations, but I firmly believe that there is very little arbitrage that exists in the long term. In today's information-rich world, you will get what you deserve, either in your current organization or in another one. Newly minted regional sales managers often benchmark their compensation to their counterparts in a larger organization, someone who has been doing the job for the last 10 years with a much larger profit and loss statement, forgetting that the organization has taken a bet in giving them an opportunity as a newbie. But if they perform and deliver over the years, is any organization going to take the decision to not pay them fairly? Very unlikely. What is due to you can only be delayed, not denied.

Too many times, people also don't take up otherwise transformational opportunities because of the monster of comparison, because they don't want to report to someone who was once their contemporary or is younger than them. The mind thinks, 'I am reporting to this person, who started working 10 years after I graduated from college!' Yet, this is increasingly becoming a reality as organizations become less hierarchical and push innovation. In fact, a CareerBuilder survey has shown that 34 per cent of people report to a boss younger than them.[2] Should Sheryl Sandberg not have taken up a chief operating officer (COO) role at Facebook because she reported to Mark Zuckerberg, who was significantly younger than her? I am often asked how I work in a situation

---

[2] Steven Rothberg, '34% of workers have younger bosses', *College Recruiter*, 19 September 2012.

where most of my direct reports are older than me, and my response is that it works when we stop making a big deal about it. Traditional hierarchy is obsolete; all of us are simply playing out our roles, and we will bring something unique to our jobs.

One of my dearest relationships at Edelweiss MF is with Dhawal Dalal, who is a veteran in the fixed income business and is significantly more experienced than I am. We argue and debate endlessly, we share vacation pictures and bond over our shared love for north Indian food in cold Delhi winters – and when I told him one Diwali that I needed him to fly to Delhi at 7 a.m. the next day because of a crisis during the Bharat Bond saga, he did it without thinking twice. I had known he would. Both of us have managed to throw the 'age difference' out of the equation and build a relationship based on trust and respect for each other's work. It's simple and it works.

In 2019, my college classmate Vaibhav Jatia, who runs a very successful hospitality business, Rhythm Realty, and I were talking about our 18-year-long relationship while watching the rains at his Lonavala hotel. Everyone in our friend circle chased the same things at 18, but gradually, he said, all of us have walked our individual paths and are finding our way. We are all still very aspirational for ourselves, still very competitive, but this competition exists without constant comparison. It is a healthier, more internalized and more sustainable form of competition. Each of us has seen highs and lows, we've had our trysts with heartaches, successes, failures, losses and disenchantments, even if they have come at different times. As the Bible tells us in Ecclesiastes 3:1–8, there is a time for everything, and everything will happen, for each of us, at its own pace.

STOP HUGGING THE BENCHMARKS THAT EXIST IN YOUR MIND AND SET YOURSELF FREE – YOU WILL SEE YOU HAVE UNDERESTIMATED JUST HOW FAR YOU CAN TRAVEL.

Speaking of pace, my father has always said that each generation should take a leap forward from the previous one. He did, when he joined the foreign service, given his background, and he hopes I will use the opportunities he gave me to propel myself forward. You cannot leap forward, however, when your legs are tied to the stones of the past and shackled by the heavy chains of comparison. Stop hugging the benchmarks that exist in your mind and set yourself free – you will see you have underestimated just how far you can travel.

CHAPTER 5

TGIF – THANK GOD I'M FLAWED

IMPERFECTION: MEET THE NEW UGLY DUCKLING

Flawsome (adjective): An individual who embraces their flaws, and knows they are awesome regardless.

WHO AMONGST US HAS NOT HAD A PROBLEM WITH our looks at some point in our lives?

My schools in both Nigeria and Italy were straight out of *Student of the Year* (or *Kuch Kuch Hota Hai*, for all those growing up in the 90s). Good-looking teenagers roamed around in designer wear, and dances and proms were the centre of school life. I looked nothing like anyone in a Karan Johar movie – 15 kilos too heavy, crooked neck, in my mother's tailored creations, wearing thick glasses with pink plastic frames and with braces adorning my teeth.

A few weeks after we moved from Delhi to Nigeria, our seventh grade history teacher asked me to read out loud a paragraph from a book to the entire class. I began reading as best I could, but I could see some of the kids smiling and, for the life of me I couldn't figure out why, since eighteenth-century American history is rarely chuckle-worthy. A few days later, I overheard some kids talking about me in the corridor and I figured out what they had found so funny. It was not what I was saying, but *how* I was saying it. My thick Indian accent was apparently hilarious, and it earned me the nickname 'Apu', after the character from *The Simpsons*, that perfect desi stereotype in the West: Bengali, an undocumented immigrant, stingy with money, a staunch vegetarian, and well-educated but working in a grocery store. I was Apu, and this was in the late 1990s, when it was perfectly normal for an American kid to ask me if being Indian meant you went to school on elephants. I hated how I sounded and I hated how I looked.

It wasn't always like that. I was raised to be fearless by my parents, who insisted I take the toughest classes in school and sit on every scary roller coaster just to get rid of fear. '*Ghabrana nahi chahiye*. Don't be scared,' was something I heard a lot from my father. I had so much confidence as a child that my mother still jokes that in some of my photos I look like an officer out on inspection duty. Being a teenager changed all of this. I wondered why I had an Indian and not a British passport like my friends, why my father worked for the government instead of running his own business, and why we couldn't afford to vacation in places others could. My mother taught in the same school that I attended. She is a tall, stunning woman. I hated when kids pointed out how ugly I looked in comparison to her. People who say Twitter trolls are tough have nothing on teenagers who want to be nasty.

Eventually, I lost the weight and my braces, but my insecurities continued pricking at me, mostly because of my neck issues. On the night of my wedding – held in an outdoor venue in January, when Delhi is freezing cold – I was standing on the stage, doing the smiling-bride-taking-pictures-with-random-people thing, when towards the end of the reception a family friend came up to me and said that even though I have an issue with my neck I should try to crank it up straight. Otherwise, *her* picture with me would look bad. That is not the only time I've faced such comments. Periodically, women at airport security checks ask why my neck is the way it is. '*Kya* problem *hai*, childhood *ka hai*?' What is the problem? Have you had it since your childhood?

This stuff gets to you, no matter how strong or successful you are. It hits your self-confidence; it makes you self-conscious. Till I was about 30, it affected me so much that I hated seeing my pictures because I was convinced I was ugly.

All of us have these stories – it's not just women. All of us have imperfections that we are embarrassed about. Unfortunately, we are constantly reminded about these so-called shortcomings and long after the voices pipe down the echoes stay in our heads. It could be a physical imperfection, a scar, a bald patch; it could be our height or weight. For many, it could be an accent, discomfort with speaking a language, or the background they come from. And, for some, it is a professional failure, a heartbreak, or an old mistake they've made. We all carry the baggage of imperfection – whether we are freshers at work or CEOs – and this baggage becomes heavier with time, even though we get used to carrying it around with a smile. In today's world, when you are trolled if a hair is out of place, you start believing life must be what you see everyone else posting on Facebook and Instagram. Sharing your scars and speaking your truth is hard. After all, '*Log kya kahenge*?' What will people say?

As mentioned earlier, in 2018 I attended a storytelling training that Captain Raghu hosted for leaders at Edelweiss. I was part of a powerful group of financial services leaders, strong and successful heads of businesses, who knew each other through common leadership meets, business victories and numbers. But when each of us had to deliver TED-style talks on that Sunday between 9 a.m. and 7 p.m., there were no business strategies, budgets and quarterly plans discussed. There was just the sharing of stories – stories of struggles to escape the drudgery of a small town, stories of insecurities of not being from a famous B-school, stories of failed family businesses. There were tales of failure, loss, guilt, fear and redemption, and, as these stories unravelled, the atmosphere in the room changed. Vulnerability built a connection among the leaders in a way spreadsheets never could have.

The atmosphere in that room gave me the confidence to narrate my story, a story that I had never had the courage to tell anyone in its entirety or even share privately with my parents or Nalin. Once it was out there, I received tremendous affection from my colleagues, even those whom I only knew formally before the talk. That gave me the confidence to share the story on a public platform (in the video that became 'The Girl with a Broken Neck'). That talk allowed me to finally let go of my baggage. I admitted my struggle with my neck and my complex about my looks, I talked about rejection and my attempt to jump off a building, and I talked about the insecurity of being a founder of a start-up and the lifestyle challenges I faced even with close friends. There were 500 people in the auditorium that day, but I was speaking, first and foremost, to myself.

Captain Raghu told me I would never imagine how far the talk would travel, and he was right – even though I didn't believe him at first. I have received thousands of messages since it went live, and I still get them today, from men and women around the world, from colleagues of my father who are in their 80s, from friends of my younger brother, from former classmates in Nigeria and from people I don't know. A guy in a fintech firm told me how the story of the fake labels stitched on my clothes in Nigeria reminded him of his insecurity about wearing unbranded clothes bought off Linking Road in Mumbai. A boy from Bangladesh sent me a picture of the defect in his right cheek and told me the talk had given him the confidence to own his disfigurement, and a girl working at a brokerage firm in Mumbai told me that perhaps now she would stop worrying about being obese. But my favourite messages are still from the fathers who said they wanted their daughters to meet me. Thanks to these messages, I felt connected to hundreds of thousands of people I had never met, and more connected to my teams, distributors, clients and peer CEOs. Did these people connect with me because I am a CEO? No. They connected to a girl with a broken neck, a real person with flaws and imperfections, just like them and everyone else.

This single video showed me how powerful it is to slowly unpeel all your layers, reveal your flaws and vulnerabilities, and be your authentic self. It took me more than 30 years to realize it, even though the plots of countless movies have taught us the same thing. One of my favourite films – and probably the best coming-of-age story the Indian film industry has produced so far – is *Jo Jeeta Wohi Sikandar*, the story of an intense rivalry between two colleges, Rajput and Model. Rajput has students who are beautiful people who are academic superstars and athletic champions; Model has the so-called losers, who never get anything right. In the final thrilling cycle race that forms the climax of the film, 99.99 per cent of the viewers who watch the movie cheer for the kids from Model. We may admire the students of Rajput, but we relate to the students of Model. We see ourselves in the plain Jane who is told she's not pretty enough, in the younger sibling who can never live up to his parents' expectations, in the guy who doesn't think he is good enough because he doesn't own a car – and when we relate to someone, we want to see them win. The reel-life victory of the underdog is the real-life victory of the vulnerable.

I have noticed that by admitting to my imperfections and vulnerabilities my conversations with others have become more real. I have had interview candidates frequently open up to me in a first conversation about the deep challenges they have faced in their past organizations or the personal issues they have combatted. My employees have shared brutally honest, personal stories because they feel a connection. Even more surprisingly, after the video aired, I have received comments and posts about how the viewers trust me more in my capacity as a money manager, even though I didn't speak a word about finance or mutual funds in it. As companies and individuals, we can produce reams of marketing about how trustworthy and reliable our brands are, but honest stories travel the distance advertising budgets cannot.

When I ask people what holds them back from talking about their vulnerabilities, the most common fear they voice is being judged or, worse, being taken advantage of. I do believe that while 5 per cent of the world will do what they have to, you will still find support from the majority. In 2020, an online publication wrote a piece on how CEOs of mutual fund companies invest, and published pictures of the six CEOs it had interviewed. In a comment, one reader decided to focus on how I have a squint visible in the photograph. He was silent on the looks of every other CEO (incidentally, all male). Rather than squirming about this tweet, as I once would have, I tweeted back, 'A squint in the eyes, a broken neck, and weight issues for years. A lot of questions as a child, some even now. And then one day, you realize you are unique and beautiful. As you are.' In response, I was swarmed with love and support, because as Monika Halan, friend and veteran journalist tweeted, 'This is every woman's story.'

The biggest benefit of accepting my vulnerabilities has been personal and internal. Confidence, when damaged, makes you insecure even when you are delivering your best. When I was 20, I took an algorithms class at UPenn with Nalin and I

CONFIDENCE, WHEN DAMAGED, MAKES YOU INSECURE EVEN WHEN YOU ARE DELIVERING YOUR BEST.

did well in it all through (I ended up being a teaching assistant the next year for the class). In our final exam, there was a question about what algorithm you would use to solve the famous car refuelling problem (essentially, your strategy for refilling a car with petrol on a long trip, while minimizing the number of stops). After the exam, Nalin and I went to meet Sampath Kannan, our professor, to discuss the exam. I was quiet throughout the conversation, convinced that I had done terribly. When the discussion came to the car problem, Nalin told Sampath how he had written a beautiful, dynamic programming algorithm to crack it. Sampath laughed, telling Nalin that he had got it wrong. The solution was much simpler – you just had to keep going till you ran out of gas. That was what I had written! I had the right answer, but I didn't have the confidence to admit it because I was scared of being wrong.

Being able to tell myself and people around me that I am not perfect has helped me discover my self-confidence. From not being able to speak even when I have had the right answer, I can now laugh through a mistake while speaking on stage or even sing with my not-so-great voice on a webinar (if only to have Prahlad Kakkar tell me I have no sense of *sur* and laugh over it!). Much of what life gives us – who our parents are, where we are born, where we grew up, what we look like – are constants. They are fixed, like the value of pi. We have no control over them. Embracing vulnerability has helped me accept and celebrate these constants, rather than running away from them or fighting to change them.

Most children have heard the story of the ugly duckling – based on the fairy tale written by Hans Christian Andersen – who, after being teased and taunted by fellow ducklings, decides to throw himself at a flock of swans, assuming he will be killed. He forgets that he has grown up and matured into a beautiful swan and is finally welcomed by his fellow swans. I hope a version of this story is rewritten, where the duckling owns his imperfections, where he understands that it's his imperfections that set him apart from his peers and make him who he is, where his happiness does not depend on becoming a swan. Who defines what 'ugly' is anyway?

YOU @ WORK: TAKE OFF THAT CAPE

'Today you are you. That is truer than true. There
is no one alive who is youer than you.'

– Dr Suess

THE CORNER OFFICE IS A POWERFUL PLACE. IT'S ALSO
supposed to be a lonely one.

As Ranveer Allahbadia reminded me when he
invited me on his podcast, the popular perception
of a CEO is an individual who is larger than
life, usually feared and intimidatingly difficult
to approach. As leaders, CEOs are also always
supposed to be in control, armed with all the
answers, corporate Superwomen or Supermen
flying around with majestic capes billowing in their
wake, carrying the pressure of saving the world on
their shoulders.

I believed this till I became one of them.

In the commencement speech she delivered at

Harvard University in May 2013, Oprah Winfrey recounted her experience of interviewing more than 35,000 people: Presidents of countries, rockstars, heroes, homemakers, and both victims and perpetrators of crimes. She says that each time, after the camera was shut off, each individual she interviewed, whether it was President George Bush or Beyoncé, asked her the same question: 'Was that okay? Did I do fine?' She reminded us that all of us are bound by a common need to be validated, to be heard. At the end of the day, everyone out there is asking, 'Do you hear me? Do you see me? Does what I say mean anything to you?' Every bit of this is true in the office as well, and whether we are in a cubicle or in the corner office, we will have difficult days and difficult years and we will want to be heard.

While most of our colleagues may be ready to listen, bringing our honest self to work may feel like a struggle. Pop culture and our conditioning subconsciously teach us that the corporate world is ruthless and demands that we look and behave in a certain way while we are a part of it, following an unwritten code that defines a corporate professional. As I learnt, trying to fit into this box can be suffocating and is unnecessary.

A year into working at Edelweiss in 2015, I had

my first miscarriage. It wasn't easy to cope with, but I jumped back into work a few days after the hospital procedures. I didn't share any information about the incident with anyone. Later that year, I had another miscarriage. The second one was far more emotionally draining, and I was told on 13 September 2015, a day before my birthday, that I would have to be hospitalized the next day. When I went to the office on 14 September, I sat in the cabin which my team had beautifully decorated and enjoyed all the celebrations, but my mind was focused on the fact that I would be spending that night in the hospital. I was emotionally agitated. My mother had left Mumbai for Delhi just that morning, and Nalin called and asked her to come back to be with me. The night of 14 September, while I was in the hospital, one of my bosses called me to wish me for my birthday and asked how I was celebrating. I couldn't hide the fact that I was in the hospital, but I just could not bring myself to talk to him or anyone else about what had happened. My boss kept asking me how he and the firm could help with the situation, and told me they were there for me in every possible way. But I just could not tell him perhaps because talking about a miscarriage has always been considered taboo.

Call it my insecurities or the fear of judgement, I felt trapped. I had an incredibly kind team and an incredibly kind boss, and yet I could not be honest and reach out to them during one of the toughest moments of my life.

Any team that aspires to build something great today will live through periods of absolute hell – some of it collective and professional, some of it personal and individual. We will see market downturns, budget gashes and layoffs; we will live through attacks from the competition and environmental changes that are out of our control and may alter our industry in unimaginable ways. We may even see parts of our business becoming completely obsolete. Even as we grapple with our professional environment, we may go through personal grief –over loved ones dying, or heartbreaks and divorces, not to mention setbacks to physical and mental health. Nothing has been a better reminder for me of this than the COVID-19 pandemic, particularly during April and May of 2021, when the second wave was at its peak in India. These are times when we should reach out and lift each other up, but how are we supposed to do that if we aren't honest with each other?

When you are trapped by the belief that 'life is

WHEN YOU ARE TRAPPED BY THE BELIEF THAT 'LIFE IS LONELY AT THE TOP', YOU ARE ALSO PLAGUED BY THE 'LONE LEADER' PROBLEM. LIFE DOESN'T GIVE YOU EXTRA CREDIT FOR DOING IT ALL YOURSELF.

lonely at the top', you are also plagued by the 'lone leader' problem. When I started in my role as CEO, because of my conditioning, I felt as though the entire burden of problems rested on my shoulders alone because of my designation, and I was scared to share problems with my team. I felt they would not be able to handle the weight of a crisis. It was not only incredibly stressful for me but suboptimal for the business.

In August 2020, an internal restructuring impacted the financials of my division. I have always been hands on with numbers, but I just couldn't wrap my head around the situation we were in or how to move forward. Asking for help was the only option. I expanded my monthly financial review – which till then had been limited to me and my chief financial officer – to include three very senior members of my team in sales, strategy and marketing, opening up every detail of the company financials with them. I actually didn't have to say much. When they looked at the numbers, they understood my situation, and jumped into action. Deepak Jain, who heads sales, focused on expanding revenue from the equity business, and Niranjan Avasthi and Rashida Roopawalla (in marketing and strategy, respectively) focused on optimizing every cost they could. They solved the problems faster and more aggressively than I could have done alone, finding solutions I would have never thought of. Deepak later told me, 'We had to jump in. It was obvious you needed help, even if you were not directly asking for it.'

In many situations and especially when you lead teams, it's natural to feel that you have to shoulder all the burdens, but life doesn't give you extra credit for doing it all yourself. When you put up an honest hand and ask for help, you will be surprised how many people come forward and how much better the outcome is. The old wisdom goes, '*Batane se samaysa aadhi hoti hai, aur khushi dugni*.' When problems are shared, their magnitude drops by half, but when joy is shared, it doubles. I have never regretted sharing my problems with my colleagues and using their help to arrive at a solution. After all, we spend 12 hours a day, five days a week together – much more than we do with our families. When women share their challenges with me, of battling tough pregnancies or having gone through miscarriage, I tell them my story. There's no shame in sharing pain or grief or difficulties, and while sharing is a personal choice, more often than not it enables people to step forward with a kind shoulder or a helping hand, making a tough phase easier.

I also believe that we need to be less harsh on ourselves when we don't have it together in the office, when our emotional side shows up in a tough situation. During my first performance review in 2015, I burst into tears and while everyone around me was very understanding, I felt guilty about it for a whole month. A voice inside my head kept telling me that my crying at work was seen as a sign of emotional immaturity, that no one would ever take me seriously again. But with the experience of managing larger teams, I have realized that people – both men and women – get emotional under different circumstances. So if you tear up once in a while – out of frustration, out of being overwhelmed by work, or when a dear colleague resigns – don't judge yourself for it.

In March 2020, when the first wave of COVID-19 infections struck, one of the industries that was hit the hardest was hospitality. Hotels looked like ghost towns, properties were being shut down and people were losing jobs by the week. At that time, the then CEO of Marriott International, the late Arne Sorenson released

AUTHENTICITY TRAVELS FURTHER THAN WE ESTIMATE AND STAYS WITH PEOPLE LONGER THAN WE IMAGINE.

a video in which he minced no words, saying that this was the worst crisis his brand had ever seen, and this is a brand that had experienced 92 years of global history, including the Great Depression, the Second World War, 9/11 and the 2008 financial crisis. In the last two minutes of the video, he teared up. He said there was nothing worse than having to close down hotels and lay off staff. 'I haven't had a tougher moment than this,' he declared.[1] When times are tough, CEOs are always under pressure to look good in front of Boards and shareholders, to project that all is well. (Sorenson was also battling cancer then and his team was concerned about what the world would think when he showed up bald in public!) But his unabashed and brutal honesty won not only a lot of love from his team but from thousands of people who commented on the video

---

[1] Arne Sorenson, 'COVID-19: A message to Marriott International associates from President and CEO Arne Sorenson', YouTube video, 20 March 2020.

and said that if they had to visit a hotel after the crisis, it would be a Marriott hotel. Authenticity travels further than we estimate and stays with people longer than we imagine.

More than once, as CEO, I have had team members call me to say that they have no purpose behind making the call, but just want to talk. I tell them it's perfectly okay as long as, in turn, on a bad day I can call them to share my frustrations without being judged. And yes, I have done so many a times and have been lucky enough to have people who've heard me out. More than once, I have been warned that I will be taken advantage of as a leader for sharing my problems with my team, and that I will not come across as 'tough enough'. My belief is that we can be demanding of teams in business but empathetic in how we deal with each other, that aggression in business and compassion for people can co-exist.

In fact, for the longest time, my corner office had a very comfortable couch, not the usual sober cream or white in colour, but a bright purple, and it became the favourite place to talk about a bad day for many people in the office. The seating arrangement has changed over the years, but the 'purple couch' has become an indelible part of our office lingo as a symbol of the power of opening up. As for me, I've realized the CEO can absolutely take off her cape, sometimes shed a tear and definitely share her load with her team. It makes the corner office a much happier place.

DIFFICULT CONVERSATIONS: JUST HAVE THEM

'When there is an elephant in the room, introduce him.'

– Randy Pausch

ONE OF MY MOTHER'S FAVOURITE QUOTES IS: 'Almost everything you need to know in life is actually taught in kindergarten.'

My mother started her career teaching in kindergarten, and even though she is now the principal of a school her favourite bunch of kids is still the kindergarteners. When two children in her class have a problem with each other and start fighting, my mother tells them to make up with a shared piece of 5 Star or KitKat. If a kid's pencil is taken away by her classmate, she simply expresses her displeasure by saying, 'I don't like what you did.' Kindergarteners are genuine and simple – they say what's on their mind, they fight and forget about it the next day and move on, they handle difficult conversations by just having them – something that we struggle with as adults.

Every workplace situation has elephants in the room – issues that are on many employees' minds, that lurk in corridors and are the centre of chai breaks – and, yet, in a large forum like an office townhall many find it difficult to raise their hands and voice them. When we find it tricky to work with a colleague, we are more than happy to write passive-aggressive emails, frequently adding people in cc simply to make our point, rather than just picking up the phone and talking through it. When we disagree with what is being said in a meeting, we struggle to speak our minds, and we stay silent when asked for feedback even when we have lots of it to give. Many of us spend years silently going through challenging relationships with bosses, often constantly blaming them in our heads, rather than addressing our differences with them. We seem to think the easiest way out is to avoid these situations altogether.

Writing about this reminds me of a lovely scene from *Dil Dhadakne Do*, a movie about a rich but obviously flawed family, where Ranveer Singh's character bursts out in the climax: '*Iss* family *mein sab upar-upar se baat kartein hain. Sach toh koi bolta hi nahi hai.*' In this family everyone just talks superficially. Not one person voices the truth.

I am a complete turtle, and have always struggled with speaking out. While I know the importance of having difficult conversations, there's still a part of me that prefers to avoid them. Until a few years ago if you asked me about my biggest weakness (and dark chocolate is not an acceptable answer!), having tough conversations was on top of the list. I hated conflict and, in fact, as Nalin still says, I actively ran away from it. He is right. If there was a difficult conversation to be had, I would postpone the meeting altogether – and I am a person who never postpones anything and is perpetually in a hurry to move ahead. Unfortunately, in a business where you not only manage a large number of people, but also deal with upset customers and fluctuating market cycles, I have had no choice but to fight my fears and have these conversations.

Remember that performance review during which I broke down? Well, for five years before that I hadn't had any performance reviews and, because of my adjustment challenges in a large organization, I entered the conversation in an agitated state of mind. That review, as I remember it, started off fine as we went through the highlights of the year, but halfway into the conversation I started getting emotional as I began to talk about the issues I had had and within a few minutes I was crying uncontrollably. My boss had no inkling of anything being wrong, because I had been too scared to have that conversation with him during our interactions through the rest of the year. Realizing it was unwise to continue the review, given my state, my boss decided to end the meeting and suggested we talk later that evening. When we did, he asked me to list out my issues and promised to solve them. Number one on that list (and I laugh about this now) was that I shared a cabin with my husband, and it was too much for two people who were married and saw each other at home anyway. 'Why didn't you tell me?' he said. 'I thought you wanted it that way. This can be fixed tomorrow!' I always look back at this conversation as a reminder that most problems are solvable; they just need to be voiced.

People may actually want to help solve our issues, but they need to be given a chance to do so. After all, no one can read your mind! It's also important to remember that people judge us much less than we think they do. Incidentally, all of us who were present at that performance review laugh about it now, and in hindsight that is how many difficult conversations end. A strong and mature association is one in which we can have these conversations without them affecting us or the relationship.

I have found that being honest is the easiest way to mend tricky relationships, not just with bosses, but also with colleagues and peers. Early on in my role as CEO, I faced a bit of a complicated situation with a senior colleague. He joined the organization in a role that structurally often conflicts with that of the CEO, and we are both headstrong and opinionated people. Work progressed and cordially so, but professionally the chemistry that would have done us a lot of good was missing.

Sometime after he joined, we went for an off-site leadership programme and were faced with an exercise where we had to identify colleagues whom we worked with closely and have an honest conversation with them – at midnight, of all times. My colleague and I spoke for an hour that night, by the poolside of a little resort in Alibaug. He shared his perception of how I treated him, and I shared mine about how he handled meetings. At the end of the discussion, he told me something I have never forgotten. He said, 'I will never do anything to make you look bad. I am only here to help.' That one hour was the turning point of our relationship, and we ended up becoming very good friends – so much so that eventually when I used to have a bad day at work, he would pop into my cabin because he knew I needed to talk. Today, I am secure in the knowledge that whenever I have a real problem, he is just one phone call away.

In the book *To Kill a Mockingbird* by Harper Lee, Atticus, the central character who is a lawyer, tells his daughter, Scout, 'You never really understand a person until you consider things from his point of view, until you climb into his skin and walk around in it.' It is a line I can never get out of my head. My father, a career diplomat, has always said dialogue is the best path to both understanding and mending relationships; without dialogue, misgivings fester. When others realize that two people don't get along, there is an inevitable tendency to take sides and take advantage of the situation. It serves no one well. Each time two teams or individuals tell me that they are struggling to work together, I ask them if they have had their version of the midnight resort chat, and usually the answer is a no. Sometimes, I have offered to facilitate these chats with that KitKat my mother uses in her classroom!

Some of the most difficult conversations are the ones that need to be had after we make mistakes – whether they are small errors or big, glorious blunders. In the mutual fund business, we sell promises more than products: the promise of future returns that may not be realized if market conditions don't favour what we do. Sometimes, despite our best intentions, we underperform and sometimes there is a mismatch of customer expectations. In either of these eventualities, we end up with upset investors and disappointed distributors.

At the time I was appointed CEO, the flagship fund of Edelweiss MF was going through a rough run performance-wise and because it was the flagship product its underperformance cast a wider shadow on the brand, agitating customers and distributors. On my first trip to Delhi, six days into the job, I drew on my inner Amitabh Bachchan swagger and told my team to set up meetings with the distributors who were giving them the roughest time. They obliged. I went into the meeting that day ready to take some flak but found myself totally unprepared for what I faced. For an hour after I entered the conference room, it felt like I was being attacked from all ends. Without a break. At the end of the hour, I decided the best thing I could do was to

admit that our performance
hadn't been good, but
reassure the customers that
we would work towards
making it better.

WHEN YOU ADMIT TO YOUR MISTAKES, RATHER THAN DENYING OR DEFENDING THEM, YOU ARE LIKELY TO GET ANOTHER CHANCE.

'I know you have trusted
us with your client's money,
and it isn't easy to do that with a younger brand.
Our poor performance puts you in a tough spot.
We know this,' I told them. I acknowledged our
mistakes, told them what we could do to improve
the situation and what we couldn't (including
fixing our performance issues quickly), and asked
for time. Fortunately, and I am grateful for this,
many of them chose to trust us that day. The fund
that was ₹250 crore in 2017 has grown to ₹7,500
crore in the five years since, is one of the largest in
the category and very much still our flagship. When
you admit to your mistakes, rather than denying
or defending them, sit people down and tell them
where you went wrong and promise to find a way
out, you are likely to get another chance. You build
trust, you build credibility.

David Kabiller, a founder at AQR, and one of
the best relationship guys I know, always says that
there is no harm in saying sorry to a client – you

will never regret it. As for your ego, Anant, my partner at Forefront, used to say, 'Let's just take our ego, put it in a glass of water, and throw that glass down. And then walk over the pieces.'

When the ego is out of the equation, you will express yourself more openly and fearlessly. I have known what it is like to not speak up in a meeting for fear of saying something that is not smart enough or of people thinking less of me. I found it even tougher when those participating in the meeting were seniors with strong opinions, people who had a lot more confidence to speak their minds. Over the years, I've learnt that speaking up matters. Asking tough questions, especially publicly, builds a safer and more open workplace and countering someone's point of view leads to productive arguments, which only help the organization.

Thankfully, I have a team that isn't afraid to make their voices heard. In 2020, we tied up with a global giant, MSCI Inc., to launch passive index funds and worked on two ideas – an Indo-global healthcare idea and a financial services idea. We launched the healthcare fund first because of market conditions and were all set to move on to the financial fund next. Launching a new product (called an NFO, or new fund offer) in the market takes significant bandwidth, especially for the marketing and sales teams, and Deepak, who heads sales at Edelweiss MF, agreed to do two NFOs back-to-back, because I had said it was important. A day after I had closed the conversation with him, Niranjan, from the marketing team, called me and said we shouldn't launch the financial fund. 'We can make a better product. The financial product isn't as strong as healthcare. Let's take time to build a better product,' he said. I was upset; I had put in so much effort to convince the team to do this, and here was Niranjan coming in at the last minute and asking for a change. Why did he have to do this at such a short notice, I told him irritably. Later, he wrote me a message: 'In any other place, I would never have spoken. But we have built an environment where we can speak our minds, and so I did.' Candour breaks down the layers of formality that exist in an organization, and the outcome is better results at work.

Research backs this up.

A few years ago, I learnt there was something called a Marshmallow Challenge, where small teams have to build a structure in 20 minutes using spaghetti, tape, strings and marshmallows. The winning team is the one that is able to construct the tallest structure, with a marshmallow at the top, within the time allotted. The idea is to collaborate quickly to complete something, and the study has produced fascinating results. Apparently, the group that performs the best, apart from architects, is kindergarten kids and the group that performs the worst is recent MBA graduates. The latter spend a lot of time managing egos and figuring out what to say to each other, the study claims; kindergarteners, on the other hand, skip status management, say things as they are and combine their energies to build the best structure.

We can learn a lot – not just about living life but also about being more productive at work – from kindergarteners. Mom was right. She usually is.

CHAPTER 6

HARD WORK × A LITTLE HELP

BEYOND HARD WORK: IMPROVE YOUR MULTIPLE

'The magic is in the doing of simple things repeatedly and long enough to ignite the miracle of the Compound Effect.'

– Darren Hardy

HOW OFTEN HAVE YOU SEEN TWO EQUALLY competent people – both driven and hardworking – join an organization at the same time but rise at dramatically different paces? Is it sheer luck, is the world of work simply unfair, or is there more to it?

I call it the impact of the 'personal P/E multiple', a lesson that studying companies has taught me about careers.

The price of a company's stock is determined by two factors – its earnings per share (EPS) and its price-to-earnings ratio (P/E ratio). EPS simply indicates how much money a company earns on each share. Consequently, it grows as the company's profits grow. P/E, on the other hand, is the ratio that measures its current share price against its EPS. It denotes the market value of the company – what multiple investors are willing to pay for every rupee of the company's earnings. It is very common in markets to see two different companies – say two banks – with very similar EPS, but trading at different prices because the market is willing to pay a higher multiple for one bank over the other. EPS is a straightforward concept to understand; it is dependent on earnings and is largely internal to the company. P/E is a little more complex because it is an external factor. The market trusts companies with relatively higher P/E multiples, because it is evident that they have done a certain set of things right and are perceived in a certain way.

Now think of yourself as stock and your career as the stock price. We spend a lot of our journey focusing on what we can call our EPS – building our earnings potential by getting a good education, joining the right company and slogging it out at work every day to fulfil our ambitions. But while hard work matters – and it absolutely does – most often it isn't enough. Our personal P/E does make a difference. How you are perceived in your organization and industry can shape the opportunities you get, and this helps multiply the impact of hard work.

While there is no science as to what drives it, I believe the same things that shape a company's P/E ratio also help build a strong personal P/E – conviction, consistency and compounding.

Let's take the example of Starbucks. I am a self-declared coffee snob, and many people of my ilk would agree that Starbucks doesn't make great coffee. Most boutique cafes in any city do a far better job of producing a good cappuccino. Yet, Starbucks remains a multi-billion-dollar franchise and a much-loved consumer brand, because when you walk into an outlet anywhere in the world you have a familiar experience waiting for you and know exactly what you are going to get – you know what you want to order, you know the process of ordering it and you know how it will taste. It could be in a mall in Dallas, in an airport in Moscow, or in the store behind the Taj Mahal Hotel in Colaba in Mumbai, but your short, tall and grande lattes, customizable with soya, skim and almond milk and different toppings, are always served as per expectations and in an environment you can relax in. Starbucks is clear that it doesn't compete

**WHY FIGHT TO
BE AN AVERAGE
PLAYER IN THE AREA
THAT IS POPULAR
AND DESIRABLE
RATHER THAN BE
OUTSTANDING AT
WHAT IS REALLY UP
YOUR ALLEY?**

on coffee but on experience, and for a certain clientele experience matters.

Having clarity and conviction about what you are and what you are not is a potent source of power, as much for brands like Starbucks as for individuals as they navigate their career. As in any industry, in the asset management business too, your career can take multiple paths – investing, sales and business, marketing or operations. Among these, investing has always been perceived to be the most glamorous. Everyone wants to pick stocks, but not everyone is cut out for it. Some of the most successful professionals I know are those who may have started as investing professionals but had the clarity and humility to admit that this is not what they excel in. They then take on a more business-oriented path, often rising to become CEOs. The question is, when there is a market for both good cappuccino and a great coffee experience, why fight to be an average player in the area that is popular and desirable rather than be outstanding at what is really up your alley?

There are definite advantages to not fighting the

popularity battle. Standing for something different is a good way to stand out. In 2017, our team at Edelweiss MF was trying to figure out how to host events for distribution partners and ensure a good turnout within our limited budget compared to larger peers – a tricky problem in an industry with 45 players where there is no shortage of extravagant events for people to attend. Asset management events tend to be fairly formal with long product pitches and data-rich presentations. We decided to abandon both. Our platform, Konnect, would run with a twist – it would be of short duration, storytelling would replace the traditional slides, investment conversations would be in the form of light-format panels and the event would end with me hosting an edgy *Koffee with Karan*-style rapidfire (aptly named 'Rum with Radhika'). That was our pitch – sharing information in an entertaining format and, most importantly, focusing on selling a product. It worked. Attendance at the event was better than our expectations in the first year, and by the second and third years we recorded a much bigger group of attendees than many of our larger peers – to the point that at

STANDING FOR SOMETHING DIFFERENT IS A GOOD WAY TO STAND OUT.

an event in Hyderabad not only were all the seats taken but there were people who stood through the entire event just to be a part of it. We now know that Konnect and our entire marketing platform can compete on content with the biggest in the business, and our aim is to make up through the quality of our content for what we do not have in marketing budgets. Making sharp choices helps your external positioning and your internal focus. As you shape your career, be clear about what your edge is and where you will compete. And then take the bold decisions and back them with conviction.

In one of the most quoted poems of all time, Robert Frost's 'The Road Less Travelled', the poet writes that when two roads diverge taking the one less travelled by (that is, the more difficult path) makes all the difference. Sure, taking the difficult turn is hard, but continuing to trudge down the road as the weather worsens and the cracks become visible is, in my book, vastly underappreciated. In a world where fashion brands change collections in three weeks and 30-second YouTube videos feel too long, being consistent is perhaps the most difficult thing to do. In doing just this, HDFC Bank stands out.

HDFC is one of India's largest banks and the unwritten understanding in the market is that

brand HDFC stands for a consistent 20 per cent
growth year-on-year with a very low probability
of major negative surprises or risks. In exuberant
stock markets, words like risk, consistency and
steadiness are less popular because investors want
fast growth. The HDFC group, however, has over
the years stuck to its mantra – scale and steadiness –
and, over time, each company that carries its brand
name, from asset management to life insurance,
has become associated with these qualities. They
usually command a P/E multiple better than their
peers. When you choose to stand for something
and make a sharp choice, remember that it will fall
out of season at some point. It happens to stocks,
it happens to industries, it even happens in the
careers of India's icons. The minute Shah Rukh
Khan delivers a few flops, or Virat Kohli doesn't
perform in a few games, there are tweets about
how they are past their prime and magazine covers
loudly proclaim that they are finished. The public
quickly finds a new favourite – think magazines
that claimed Hrithik Roshan had dethroned Shah
Rukh Khan in 2000 after just one blockbuster.

Time constantly tests our convictions. I manage
money managers for a living, and if there is one
certainty in this profession it is that fund managers,

no matter how good they are at what they do, will go through periods in which they don't perform. It's a law of financial gravity – each manager has a different style, and different styles do well in different environments. Since markets are cyclical, each style has a period when it is out of favour.

When I started out, during the times when fund performance was tough I would get extremely agitated with the team – unintentionally joining a queue of investors, distributors and media in giving them a hard time. At this time, a friend who has been a money manager for over 20 years told me that if you perform badly one year, your entire career feels as though it is up for a review. It was then that I realized the need to be countercyclical. I needed to create an environment that would encourage the team to stick to their convictions and ride out the bad times, because they were certain to bounce back when the current cycle was done. There is a difference between bad times and bad performers, and even the best of performers fall on times when nothing seems to work for them. But because so few people hold on to their beliefs during these times, those who stick it out are seen as creating serious value.

Ask the single malt industry. On a trip to a single

malt distillery in Scotland, a distiller told me that while mixing malts itself is a very quick process, much of the flavour of any malt comes from it simply sitting in a cask over many years. As the malt ages, it endures different conditions and seasons, gets infused with the flavours of the cask and in time acquires a valuable maturity. It's no wonder that at this distillery a bottle of 12-year-old malt is sold for $40, an 18-year-old one for $80, while a bottle of a 25-year-old single malt is worth nothing less than $2,000!

This almost magical force, which works on both markets and malts, is called compounding. I believe that over time if you do something with enough conviction and consistency you achieve what I term as career compounding. As you go along, more and more people start noticing what you do and associating you with that idea or quality or skillset, and small actions can catapult into a larger force. In 2011, two years after starting Forefront, we were on the lookout to induct a few smart interns because we couldn't afford any real employees. The M&T programme at UPenn, of which I am an alumnus, had an internship programme for students at companies run by its former students. So we put up an internship post saying that we were looking for interns to join our investment start-up in Mumbai while also mentioning that we couldn't afford to pay them anything. M&T interns are sought out by the best global companies, who pay them top dollar, so we were pretty sure no one would apply. Surprisingly, we got an application. This was an intern whose home was in Mumbai, and I suspect he applied mostly because the industrial estate our office was located in was five minutes away from his house, which meant he could go home for lunch every day. He ended up spending 10 weeks with us and did a fairly good job. The next year, we put out a post for two slots. This time, we received 10 applications, surprisingly from some who were not of Indian origin. We chose two, including an Asian American, who had no connection to India at all. In the third year, we opened the programme for three slots, and this time received 50 to 60 applications. This meant that half the eligible class of first and second year M&T students were applying to intern at an unknown start-up in Mumbai, which by now could afford to give them a small housing allowance but was still far from paying top dollar. By the fourth year, we had other Ivy League colleges contacting us for internships.

From then on, year after year, we had top-tier

talent from M&T, students of American, European, Korean and Chinese origin, slogging it out through 14-hour days with us, struggling with the demands of living through Mumbai's monsoons in a pre-Ola, pre-Uber world. By then, everyone was asking us what the secret sauce was – why were these students choosing us when they potentially had better brand options to intern with? The short answer to that is we had a clear story that compounded on campus. By virtue of being a start-up, a Forefront intern would be working directly with one of us co-founders on building an investment strategy where real money would be put to work in the following months, rather than a corporate project that faced the possibility of never being implemented at a large financial services firm. The programme competed on experience rather than traditional metrics and it delivered this experience year-on-year. It found a loyal audience for those who sought this kind of challenge, and over the years as interns went back and narrated their experiences on campus, the story and appeal of the programme acquired a life of its own. Had we imagined any of this would happen when we got the first intern? No. Did we underestimate the value of compounding? Yes.

I started writing regularly on social media

platforms in 2017, using Twitter and LinkedIn to
share small life and work stories inspired by day-
to-day events. Two interesting incidents occurred
in November 2020. In the first week of the month,
I was ranked at number 40, by *Fortune* magazine
on a list of the top women in Indian business, a few
ranks behind Priyanka Chopra at 36. A few days
later, the folks at LinkedIn listed my name among
the Top 20 voices in India and also as one of the
Top 10 voices in the world in banking and finance.
I was one of two Indians on that list, the other
being Raghuram Rajan, the former governor of the
Reserve Bank of India. That was it! I was convinced
I was a fraud. How could anyone list my simple
posts in the same category as posts written by a
person of Mr Rajan's stature? I decided I wouldn't
tell anyone about my LinkedIn listing, but couldn't
escape from my parents, whom I was living with
during the lockdown months of the first wave of
the COVID-19 pandemic. Characteristically, my
mother laughed when I told her of my concern
about the lists. 'What's wrong with you? Why are
you comparing yourself to Priyanka Chopra and
Raghuram Rajan? You have your own style, and
your own audience, and they have theirs,' she told
me. 'What you do, they don't; and what they do,

you don't.' That day, I learnt a little bit about the power of doing something authentic and believing in it – even if it is simple and different from everyone else. My honest

TELL YOUR STORY, TELL IT WITH CONVICTION, AND DON'T STOP TELLING IT.

expressions and reflections, written with some consistency, had compounded into a certain kind of meaningful recognition. This, I believe, is the story of many of the opportunities I have got.

Whether it's an individual or a company, each one of us is out there trying to sell our story, and the P/E multiple is the world's way of telling us, 'We trust you.' In my start-up days, I had a long debate with a veteran investment banker on what the right business model for a financial services start-up is. At the end of a few hours, he said, 'Radhika, if you want my take, finally, the business model doesn't matter so much. Just pick one that makes sense to you. And be at it long enough. That matters much more.'

That's good advice from a man who values companies for a living. Tell your story, tell it with conviction, and don't stop telling it. The process of compounding will kick in, and just as companies find their investors, you will find your listeners.

NETWORKING: EARN THE SPECIAL DIVIDEND

'The opposite of networking is not working.'
— Someone smart

IN APRIL 2017, THREE MONTHS INTO MY CEO ROLE at Edelweiss MF, I went to my first industry conference, a large one attended by CEOs, industry professionals, distributors and the media. I was looking forward to it because it was my first chance to get to know my peers and potential clients. In a formally draped silk saree and armed with business cards, I made my way to a packed conference room at the hotel in which it was being held. It took me less than five minutes to figure out two things: one, I knew no one in the room, and two, they all knew each other.

There was a warmth and camaraderie in the room that was comforting for an insider but intimidating for an outsider. Since I was too scared to talk to anyone, I spent most of my time walking around aimlessly, pretending to be busy on my phone (having that device handy was really helpful!), waiting for the event to start. Edelweiss MF was not highlighted in any way that evening, unlike our peers, and I was secretly relieved – at least I didn't have to talk to anyone. Of course, not being mentioned at all made me feel irrelevant, but the scarier thought was what would happen when the event ended and the cocktails began. I would actually have to talk to people then! It was a terrifying thought; so terrifying that as soon as the event ended, I found the closest exit and bolted out. That evening, I literally ran away. In a business where it is important to know people, many of them difficult to access, I gave up an opportunity for no good enough reason. It was a stupid thing to do.

A few years later (by which time I had settled into the industry well enough not to run away from events), I was speaking at a similar conference at another hotel and, as usual after the formal event, the cocktail hour started. It was a Friday night, Mumbai was witnessing torrential rains, and people hung around a little longer than usual to avoid getting stuck in traffic and have a good time with their peers. At the buffet counter, I noticed a youngish woman. I caught her glancing around the room and then back into her phone, looking rather lost. I went up to her and asked her if everything was okay. She was surprised and, after fumbling a bit, told me, 'I'm new to this industry. I thought I would come here and meet people. But how do I begin talking to anyone?'

Oh, I knew that feeling, as I suppose we all do. Everyone says networking is important, but for most of us it is much harder than our actual work. How do you approach people you don't know, especially those who appear inaccessible? Why should anyone talk to you when you are irrelevant to them? In a room where people are effortlessly moving in and out of circles, how do you break into a circle knowing that you will be accepted?

It took me a while to understand that although networking is important it does not mean working the room at cocktail parties (that is simply being social). Having a network is about knowing the people who exist beyond your immediate professional sphere of work (your boss, team, peers) and building meaningful relationships with them. This sounds easy and obvious, but very few of us invest time doing it.

When we start our careers, transitioning into fulfilling the demands of work is hard enough. In my first five years, I remember spending all my time either on day-to-day work or special projects, never bothering to speak to industry colleagues beyond McKinsey or AQR. In fact, I didn't even bother to explore the wider ecosystem in a large global organization like McKinsey. It was only when we started Forefront that I realized how much we needed to lean on people – especially because none of us three founders had ever worked in India before. From little things like working with regulators and setting up an office, to guidance on how to crack distribution and how to raise capital, we needed help, and a lot of it. And help had to come from people who genuinely cared about us and would make time for it; Google wasn't going to find us these people.

Unfortunately, starting to network when you need to leverage a network is extremely ineffective. HR departments across companies have a joke that you should be alert when employees start becoming active on LinkedIn, because that's a sure-shot sign they are hunting for a job. People update their profiles, start posting articles and connecting with others, hoping to make their presence felt on the

> **IF YOUR EDUCATION IS THE BEST INVESTMENT YOU WILL MAKE IN THE FIRST 20 YEARS OF YOUR LIFE, A MEANINGFUL SET OF RELATIONSHIPS IS THE BEST INVESTMENT YOU WILL MAKE IN THE NEXT 20.**

network when it is already too late. You can't ask anyone to do something for you when they hardly know you and you hardly know them, and when you haven't done anything for them first. Networks have to be seeded and grown. If your education is the best investment you will make in the first 20 years of your life, a meaningful set of relationships is the best investment you will make in the next 20.

A lot of us have mental blocks which cause us to think networking makes us seem opportunistic and self-promotional. But I believe that networking does not detract from our work – rather, it is accretive. No business operates in a silo, and having wider access and perspective will only make you a richer professional. As for not having enough time, most of us invest less of it in our relationships than what we spend watching our favourite poison on Netflix – and to very good effect.

A classmate of mine from UPenn runs a family office and a venture capital fund and is superbly 'well-networked', if that is a term. He is also an extremely shy person – a sharp contrast to the image of the outgoing charmer we all have, someone who works the room. He says the roots of building good relationships are in this adage and the actions we have traditionally learnt from our parents and grandparents, '*Neki kar, dariya mein daal.*' Do, without expecting anything in return.

Wharton professor Adam Grant taught us that the world is divided into people who are either 'net givers', those looking to help others with introductions and knowledge, and 'net takers', those looking to extract as much from others as they can for themselves. If you can do things for net givers, who will pay it forward, you will build a circle of goodwill and that will become your network. People may not immediately help you in turn, but over time you will accumulate enough goodwill, which will come in handy. We also underestimate the opportunities we get to build this kind of goodwill, in the little things we can do for people that leave a lasting impression.

A friend of mine, for instance, is constantly bombarded with requests, because of his experience with college admissions in the US, to guide other people's children through the process, and I have never seen him turn down a call for help. 'I will never say no to helping someone's kid,' he tells me. Can you always step up when someone asks you for help? No. But you can tell the other person, 'I tried my best, and I'm sorry I just can't make this happen.' These words show that you honestly tried, and that is much more than many people do.

An interesting myth about relationship building is that you have to 'seek out the most powerful person in the room', especially in the context of industry or campus networking events. Except, the most powerful person in the room is usually surrounded by people and is well aware that those flocking around want something from him or her. It's what my networked friend calls the 'mistake of only making friends with people who work at Merrill Lynch' – a reference to a time at UPenn when the company was one of the most desirable Wall Street employers. Relationship building can start anywhere and, in fact, the least intimidating person in the room may hold the key to what you want. In company presentations on campus, for instance, this could be the head of HR, whom students often ignore in their bid to talk to the CEO or senior management. They forget that heads of HR know just as much about the company as the CEO, perhaps more so, and are key to the hiring process as well. As my networker buddy says, 'Don't wait for a network to come by; build a network among the people around you.' Remember, you never know where life takes anyone and, in any case, Merrill Lynch doesn't exist today!

I also believe that just like love is often found in the most unexpected places, great relationships are formed in places where there is no explicit pressure to network. A few years after moving to India, I went to a UPenn alumni dinner, where I met Ramanan Raghavendran, a fellow alumnus, who asked me to help him build the alumni club for the 1,000-odd UPenn alumni in Mumbai. As the founding president of the club, I ended up speaking to a lot of alumni, asking them to join events and help organize them. In the process, I built relationships I otherwise would not have at a regular cocktail party.

Our alma maters and industry bodies give us many such opportunities, and while they seem like a lot of work with unclear tangible benefits, they are an easy way to widen your relationships in a setting that is familiar. Social networks, too, are your friends if you are shy, because they let you put word out about your work and enable you to connect with people without the pain of explicit rejection that happens in-person. Without Twitter, I can't think of how I would have connected with someone like Guneet Monga, for instance, who comes from the film world and is someone I have always admired. Nothing external stops a young analyst from putting out interesting content on social media today, and chances are that if it is good content it will find its way and its due. More than once, I have seen CEOs hire young people because they have been impressed by a few of their tweets!

A few years ago, a member of my personal advisory board (more on that later) asked me to moderate an event for the Indian Police Foundation, featuring a panel of eight speakers from government-affiliated organizations such as the NITI Aayog, the legal world, policy heads of social media outfits and security professionals. I flew to Delhi at a time when I was swamped both personally and professionally, and a lot of people asked me why someone in the money management business was at a police foundation event. I told them I was doing it because my advisor said I should and I don't say no to him. It ended up being a great day and not just because of the panel; I met eight people from totally different worlds and stayed in touch with some of them.

Years later, while I was deep into work on Bharat Bond, we interacted with multiple departments in the government very closely on the approvals for the product. A week before a very critical approval I was told I had to fly to Delhi to meet one particular department and that this meeting could make or break the deal. I flew to Delhi on a day's notice. I was nervous because my meeting was with a cabinet secretary equivalent and his team, and because the stakes were so high. When I walked into the room, the first person I saw was someone who had been on the panel at the police foundation event. Instantly I felt better and more in control. I had a good meeting and we soon got the green light. Two disconnected events came together to build a bridge, a network, as they often do in ways we cannot predict.

In the world of money, stocks pay dividends, a pay out to shareholders based on surplus profits. Dividends don't show up immediately, because it takes time to build up enough reserves to pay them, and often when they are paid out they aren't that huge. In fact, some companies hardly pay them. Once in a while, however, you will receive a surprise credit in your bank account from a company that usually doesn't pay dividends, but has decided to make a large payout. In markets we call this a special dividend. Effective networking reminds me of dividends. If you invest in relationships silently and consistently, without expecting great returns, you never know when it will bring a special dividend your way.

ADVISORY BOARDS: BUILD YOUR TRIBE

'If you want to go fast go alone; if you want to go far go with others.'

– African proverb

OUR COOK IN NIGERIA WAS A YOUNG IGBO (A TRIBE IN that area) and she had no shortage of problems. But she also had infinite optimism. 'My community is there,' she would say, referring to her tribe, and she told us that if she were ever in trouble and needed them, they would surely come to her rescue and help her. And they did. It could be a financial problem, a death in her family, or her young child needing to be looked after in the village while she worked in the city – her community was always there to extend a hand when she needed it.

In the late 1990s, when I lived in Lagos, Nigerians had a lot to complain about on the surface. Petrol queues lasted for days (in a country that was a major oil exporter), traffic jams – lovingly called 'go-slows' – put Bengaluru's much reviled traffic snarls to shame, and the national electricity board, the Nigerian Electric Power Authority (NEPA), was nicknamed 'Never Expect Power Again' because of the constant and sustained power cuts people had to suffer. Yet, when you landed at Murtala Muhammed International Airport in Lagos, you saw a sign that read, 'Welcome to the happiest place on earth'. In a 2011 Gallup poll of 53 countries, Nigeria earned 70 points on optimism. In comparison, Britain earned -44. The incredible optimism Nigerians possess despite not having much comes from a deep faith in the power of the community, a belief that they are one and are there for each other when required. It's no wonder the popular saying, 'It takes a village to raise a child', is actually a translation of the Igbo phrase, '*Oran a azu nwa*'.

A solid career may not need a whole village to come together, but it definitely gains from receiving some help. My father tells me that if there is one thing he wishes he had more of when he was younger, it is guidance. Many of his batchmates had parents in the civil services, but he came from a much humbler background, with no knowledge of the bureaucracy. He ended up taking the UPSC exam a few years later than his counterparts, because he didn't know the right coaching classes to take and whether to work after his master's degree or jump straight into exam preparation. In the government, where your incoming age influences the seniority at which you retire, this was important. Like him, each of us grapples with the need for advice at various stages in our career. Should I join this firm or that? Should I continue in a job even though I am unhappy with it? Should I focus on the nature of my experience or on money? Is this the right organization for me? When should I take a break from work?

I am much more fortunate than my parents were, but I have also learnt that you cannot restrict yourself to family and friends when it comes to seeking out career advice. Today, many of us work in careers that were never even an option for our parents or that simply didn't exist when they came of age. I remember feeling this way when I was choosing between a technology-oriented career at Microsoft and a consulting role at McKinsey, and then when I made the transition from consulting to finance. No one had really had a corporate career in my family, and from my parents' point of view my choices simply sounded like two similar companies that were paying a 22-year-old very good money. Friends are an even trickier lot to navigate. When we are younger, everyone is fighting for the same job, making honest conversations hard. And, in many cases, as well intentioned as they are, friends are often just as inexperienced as you. So, at the crucial point when you are looking for intervention, to whom do you turn?

The corporate answer to this is a six-letter word: Mentor. I receive nearly 10 emails a day from young people asking if I could mentor them. Somewhere in these long emails is the belief that finding a mentor is the one formula that will make their career path ahead the smoothest it can be. Most modern organizations set up mentoring programmes and most community networks have them but, as good as they sound, data suggests that their outcomes are mixed, at best. While some mentees report tangible outcomes and a few get extremely lucky, most report little benefit. Unless the programme is very well-structured, often mentors and mentees don't know where to start or what to do with each other. Plus, it is difficult to sustain the energy that a one-to-one relationship requires over any medium-term time frame. What you get, according to *Harvard Business Review* is, 'marginal or mediocre mentoring'.[1] In my case, and from conversations I have had with many senior professionals, I know I am not alone in encountering this problem – one of the biggest roadblocks is the sheer time and responsibility required to seriously mentor someone. Taking on a mentee is an enormous commitment, since you are responsible for their growth and ultimate success. Now, given the busy day jobs that most mentors have, it's not an easy responsibility to take on. In her book *Lean In,* Sheryl Sandberg writes that people turn to their mentors as knights in shining armours, who come riding in on a horse and whisk them away from their career-related problems.[2] That's a great wish to have, but most of us can hardly sign up to be the knight in someone else's lives when we are just about handling our own!

There is something to learn about a simpler approach to career success and relationships from (who else but?) Bollywood superstar Shah Rukh Khan, or SRK. In the movie *Dear Zindagi,*

[1] W. Brad Johnson, David G. Smith and Jennifer Haythornthwaite, 'Why your mentorship program isn't working', *Harvard Business Review*, 17 July 2020.

[2] Sheryl Sandberg, *Lean In: Women, Work, and the Will to Lead,* Knopf: New York, 2013.

after a break-up with her boyfriend, Alia Bhatt's character Kaira, asks Dr Jehangir (played by SRK), her therapist, whether a perfect relationship, 'that one special soulmate', exists. He responds, 'Why just one relationship? Why can't we have a special relationship that is about shared musical tastes, and another one that is about getting coffees together, and yet another that is a special intellectual relationship? Why do we put the burden of all these relationships on one single romantic relationship?'

At the workplace too, rather than seek a single mentor, I believe there is greater benefit in learning from the expertise of multiple people who contribute individually and differently to our journeys. Collectively, I call this group a 'personal advisory board'. People have so many different perspectives on advice, but for me, the 'personal' in 'personal advisory board' comes first. This is not a group I put on a website or advertise on a résumé; nor is it a group that has to meet to have intense boardroom discussions. Rather, it's a group of six or seven people who inhabit different worlds, whom I can turn to for help, are willing to lend a hand when I need it, and are brutally honest when I need them to be. I haven't sought these people out asking them to specifically be on my advisory board – they have organically made their appearance at different stages of my life and left indelible impressions. There is no pressure to measure the amount of time I spend with them, no mandatory monthly meetings (or quarterly or annual get togethers), and no standard update I have to prepare for them. Yet, I end up speaking to most of them once in every six months, and most of them are sufficiently updated on my life. My advisory board came together when I was 35, and while this stuff is talked about in the context of CEOs and leaders, I wish I had done it right in my 20s. As you rise through the ranks, you find more resources more easily – your firm may sponsor coaching, professional networks open up, you join CEO clubs, etc. – but in your confused 20s, a group like this can be invaluable.

A good personal advisory board should be diverse. When we started Forefront, we had a small advisory board for the firm. One of them is Shailesh Haribhakti, who runs one of India's largest audit firms and sits on the board of many prominent Indian companies. He brought with him a perspective on building a business with a certain set of values and governance that was very powerful. Ramanan Raghavendran, whom I have mentioned earlier, is a venture capitalist, and because we shared the same alma mater, he told us things as they were, without tacking on any frills. The two were as different from each other as apples and kiwis, but their collective wisdom made for a good fruit salad.

I've also benefited from having advisors who are from a totally different age bracket from mine and also from far outside the corporate world. The more time you spend in any company or industry, the more internally focused you become, and it is easy to get trapped in a bubble. Outsiders can give you a powerful sense of perspective. When I did the 'The Girl with a Broken Neck' talk, I was introduced to Manish Joshi who works at Josh Talks. Manish is much younger than me and comes from the world of digital media and influencers. He's been a mentor to many leading YouTubers today. He introduced me to a network completely outside my regular one, and much of my knowledge of social media, content creation and communicating with younger audiences come from him.

All of us have people in our lives whom we have grown up idolizing and looked up to, and it's natural to want them on our advisory boards. Unfortunately, they are usually out of reach. An advisory board, if it is to take off, has to be realistic, and this means a combination of three things – it must be aspirational, accessible and assertive. Aspirational is obvious; you want advice from people you respect, but they don't have to be your icons or people you want to mirror. Anyone who you think you will learn something from, who is driven to learn and better themselves, is a good candidate here. Accessibility matters, because when you need critical feedback and advice, they should have the time for you. A lot of smart and successful people are very busy, or don't want to share what they have, and a single half-hour conversation with someone doesn't make them an advisory board member.

One of the ways to get a mix of aspirational and accessible is to look at people five or 10 years ahead of you in your career, not 15 and 20. Not only are these people more likely to be easily reachable, but their perspective on problems might hit closer home. Finally, draw in people who are assertive. Giving criticism is sometimes harder than taking it, and I've met a fair share of people who will – regardless of what you do – always say pleasant things, because they don't like sharing bad news. This doesn't help at all.

In 2018, I gave an interview to a tough journalist and, for some reason every answer I gave came through as 'I said' and 'I did', rather than 'we said' and 'we did', referring to the broader team. Most people praised me for handling the journalist well, but one of the members of my advisory board told me that as a leader I shouldn't have so many 'I's in my answers. When I tried to argue that it came out this way because I felt pressurized by the journalist, he told me handling pressure elegantly was a part of my job. Since then, I think twice about what I say in every media interaction and also make sure I read the transcript of interviews before they are published. I was lucky to get this guidance early on in my role as CEO, since interacting with the media is a big part of the job.

If you want to maximize your chances of getting advice from someone, being specific can really help. No one has a great answer to requests like 'please guide me in my career' or 'please give me some advice'. People find it easier to answer when you ask for help with a specific question or with a particular skill. When I meet people, I try to focus on what they are really good at and what makes them stand out, and then I think about how I can ask them for help in that particular area. Eventually, some of them have become the go-to people on my personal advisory board for that space. I have worked with an individual who has incredible executive presence; he can walk into a room and immediately command respect, he can settle a dispute within a few minutes, without raising his voice even once, just because of the way he carries himself. I've also had a boss who is outstanding at people management, and even though we don't work together today I have made a promise to myself that I will call him when faced with a people issue. It's important to also remember that in the demanding lives that people lead today, chemistry matters. People choose to advise those in whom they see a spark. Nobody wants to spend time talking to someone who is negative or drains them of their energy by talking about their issues all the time.

Six months after 'The Girl with a Broken Neck' released, a girl who had completed the Chartered Financial Analyst (CFA) programme showed up to meet me. I was surprised because we didn't have an appointment. My assistant told me that the girl had called and pursued her with such passion that I simply had to meet her now. When we met, she gave me a card and told me about her aspirations in the finance sector and how my talk had impacted her. Her card ended with the sign-off, 'The Girl from Varanasi'. Her ambition, her spunk and her persistence struck a chord, and we have kept in touch – she writes in when she needs advice and I help her; she drops a note when something happens in my life that she hears about and I write back. A relationship now exists between us.

One of the basic principles of money management is asset allocation – combining different types of investments in your portfolio, such as equities, debt and gold, rather than holding a single one. Each of the three is individually a good asset, but because they do well at different points in time, when you combine them, you get a portfolio that is robust; one that delivers higher upside with lower volatility. The results almost feel like magic. A personal advisory board works the same way. Each individual advisor is an asset with their own value, but collectively they are a portfolio of wisdom and support that carry you through your career. And sometimes, even if they may not have all the answers, just knowing that you have a community of assets to count on is a source of confidence.

As a child, I never understood how our Nigerian cook could remain so optimistic. But I understand it now. She knew that she had her personal advisory board when she needed help. And when it mattered, they never failed to deliver.

CHAPTER 7

CHOOSE YOUR SKY, LEARN TO FLY

WORK–LIFE BALANCE: GET OFF THE SEE-SAW

'I've learnt that you can't have everything and do everything at the same time.'

– Oprah Winfrey

IS IT BETTER TO WORK 14-HOUR DAYS OR 18-HOUR days?

In July 2017, the Council of Financial Planners (COFP) asked me to speak at their retreat for financial advisors in Bengaluru on the topic 'work–life balance'. It was one of my first speaking events, so I excitedly called my mother to tell her about it. When she heard the topic, she was amused.

'You, of all people, *you*, are speaking on work–life balance? What are the organizers thinking?' she asked.

I have to admit that she had a point. I was that person who believed that working 17-hour days was better than working 15 – the proud product of a business school where we compared hours worked per day and week in different jobs with an exaggerated sense of machismo and ascribed labels based on it. Investment bankers worked 18-hour days, so they were considered 'hardcore', and consultants worked 14-hour days, so consulting was seen to be for those making a lifestyle choice. Of course, in this scenario, the laziest lot were the traders; they worked only 12-hour days. To us, how long we worked represented how much drive we had, and working ourselves to the bone was worn as a badge of honour. One of my best friends in college, Mary Obasi, once said in frustration that there is no end to this contest among the 'topper types'. 'One of you will say that you have slept only four hours. Another one will say that they haven't slept the whole night. I'm waiting for someone to say they haven't slept the whole semester and starved while doing it. Why do you take so much pride in not sleeping and not eating?' she had asked, exasperated.

I know workaholism intimately. One day, while working on a project with McKinsey in Seattle, I realized at 1 p.m. that I had developed a severe issue with my leg and could barely sit, let alone walk. I continued working, didn't tell anyone that I was in pain and walked into a hospital emergency room that night only once I'd wrapped up work. I was told I needed a minor surgery. I was alone, in an alien city, when I got the surgery done and instead of resting the next day like I was asked to, I went straight back to the office. This, despite the doctor telling me that I needed to prop my leg up for recovery. Looking back, I can see that what I did was extremely foolish – and what was even more so was the fact that I was proud of what I had done.

If you ask my parents about my single biggest weakness, they will say that for the longest time in my life I didn't know how to balance my personal life with my work life. So I had to think hard about what I would say at the COFP talk. I used the prep period to ask myself questions – about the hours I worked, the life I lived and what really made me happy. What I discovered about myself and corporate structures at large in the short span of time has stayed with me.

In my view, work–life balance is a broken concept. The idea became popular in the 1970s in the US, when a large number of women entered the workforce; till then, work and life had been seen as separate worlds. Gradually, the term started figuring in surveys and boardrooms, and it now translates to a literal count of how many hours we spend at work versus the time we spend living our lives. When I hear the term 'work–life balance' the picture I see is of a person standing at the centre of a see-saw plank, constantly trying to balance both ends. It's hard enough to do a great job at work, give meaningful time to your family and have hobbies, but do we need the added pressure of balancing this at a perfect 50–50? Why should we be so hard on ourselves, and why do we always need to have it all together?

I believe a meaningful career, a meaningful family life and meaningful hobbies are all beautiful things, and they demand different things from us at different times. Give them each the time they deserve when they require it, and during that time don't feel guilty about not giving enough time to the others. There is no point in feeling guilty about being a bad spouse when you are trying to do your best at work or about not taking on extra work when you are spending time with your family. In short, do not seek work–life

DO NOT SEEK WORK–LIFE BALANCE. BE CONTENT WITH WORK–LIFE HARMONY. THAT'S WHAT WORKS SUSTAINABLY IN THE LONG TERM.

balance. Be content with work–life harmony. That's what works sustainably in the long term.

There are times when your job will demand the world from you. A special project, a new role or a difficult boss who causes teething trouble may create a situation in which you need to give work that extra attention, maybe even put in 18-hour days once in a while. In 2011, at Forefront, we won a large mandate with one of India's big wealth management companies to launch a new product in a very short time. We knew it would be a game changer if we could deliver the product, but the timelines were very tight. For two months, Anant, Nalin and I, along with two interns, worked till 2 or 3 a.m. every night. On some nights we simply crashed in the beanbags strewn around the office and were supplied food by Anant's loving joint family. When we finally delivered for our client, and on time, it was such a triumph – even though we were completely exhausted! Similarly, the launch of Bharat Bond was so intense that I did 50 round trips to Delhi in a year, often at a couple of hours' notice.

There are also times when we have to stand up for 'life' outside of work. I have often found it hard to do this but I am learning to do more and more of it. In Europe, where I attended high school, holidays were cherished. August was sacrosanct for the Italians and people took the whole month off, no questions asked. In the US, UK, and even in Australia and New Zealand, you will struggle to find a few people at work during the Christmas–New Year period. On the other hand, in India, most of us quietly sacrifice holidays, including festivals and family time, for work that can be pushed back fairly easily. Perhaps this stems from an innate competitiveness to outdo everyone else even at the cost of our holidays, or perhaps it is a belief that taking time off will be seen as 'shirking' work. Whichever it is, we need to respect personal space – our own and others' – and learn to speak up about it.

My family is not very religious, but Diwali is special for us. Dad insists we celebrate it in all its glory every year as a family and we try to follow that as a tradition. A few years ago, a client demanded I attend a meeting that was scheduled to end late in the evening on Chhoti Diwali, when everyone knew it was not essential that we hold the meeting specifically on that day. Others in the team were also asked to participate and were silently upset about working late that day. In the end, I politely asked for the meeting to be moved to the following week, because I knew nothing would suffer if it was delayed by a few days. While seniority makes it easier to make such requests, all of us should stand up for the time we need to invest in our personal lives.

I was two years into my job at AQR, in 2008, when Nalin and I decided to get married. I needed three weeks off because we had planned 10 days of both Christian and Hindu celebrations spread across two cities, and neither Nalin nor I lived in India. People don't usually take this kind of time off for weddings in the US, at least in the finance world, and my boss was surprised when I asked for leave. He told me that when one of the partners at the firm had got married, he came to office in a tuxedo to work on the afternoon after the ceremony. However, when I explained my situation, he was very understanding – so much so that he asked me to create a separate email ID that my colleagues could use to contact me in case of a crisis, which would ensure that I wouldn't spend my entire time away checking my Blackberry. January 2008 was a chaotic month for financial markets, but I got only one emergency email in the three weeks I was away. When you build trust with your bosses and colleagues, they will reciprocate it. Often, we hesitate to ask because we are more scared of outcomes than we should be and harder on ourselves than people are on us. There are organizations that are not so empathetic, and ones where taking a vacation or having a hobby is genuinely looked down upon. It is for you to identify what kind of culture you want to be a part of as you make choices in your career.

A young graduate recently asked me on Twitter if a corporate career is worth the sacrifices it demands. While everyone has a different answer for that, I believe that life without work is incomplete. Just as my family has been there for me when work has been very tough, work has, in turn, provided strength, and even distraction, when my personal life has been less than kind. I bounced back from two back-to-back miscarriages quickly because I had a job that I loved. My opportunity to become CEO came shortly after my second miscarriage, and today my doctor and I discuss how life opens one door when another one closes.

We, especially women, take a lot of pressure on ourselves because the world constantly asks us how balanced our lives are. In a panel we were on together, Ameera Shah, CEO of Metropolis Healthcare, one of India's biggest diagnostic labs, who had just become a mother then, said that work–life balance is one of the silliest topics women are asked about. Of course, it is tough. Of course, there

WHY NOT SWAP A QUEST FOR PERFECTION WITH ONE FOR PEACE AND GIVE OURSELVES A BREAK?

are days when we are less-than-perfect wives and mothers and caregivers to older parents, days when we get very annoyed at our family, and days when we feel like having a meltdown in the office. But everyone is going through it, both women and men, so why is the expectation of balance put on a woman's head alone? Why not swap a quest for perfection with one for peace and give ourselves a break?

In 2019, I won a *Business Today* award for being one of India's '30 Most Powerful Women in Business' and when I came back from the award ceremony, my phone was ringing off the hook, with messages of congratulations pouring in. But I didn't answer any of those calls for a while, because my live-in help (the reason my house functions as efficiently as it does) was going on leave and I was scrambling to find someone to replace him. At one point, Nalin asked me to stop worrying about the house and just celebrate the moment. 'The domestic help issue will be resolved and it is okay if the house isn't perfect for a day,' he said, 'but this night isn't coming back. Calm down and smell the roses.'

One of the lessons I have learnt from the work-from-home and webinar era of the pandemic years is that work and life are much more closely tied than we think. Harmony can exist, but it doesn't need to look like a picture-perfect painting. A dog can bark and a kid can show up in the background of a video call, we can take the time to accompany a sick parent to a doctor on a weekday or run an errand, and then have a meeting on a Saturday, because a client demands it. Hours and days of the week don't define the boundaries; flexibility and fungibility are real and good.

One day in June 2020, during the first lockdown in India, Nalin and I were both at home without our help, expecting the crucial delivery of a gas cylinder between 2 and 2.30 p.m. Both of us had critical video meetings – Nalin with a foreign investor and I with a senior government official – but someone had to answer the intercom and open the door in the middle of their video call. After an elaborate negotiation, we agreed that I would open the door, which meant I had to tell the senior official in the middle of the meeting that I needed to step away to get my gas cylinder. He laughed in response. 'We're all in the same boat. Don't worry,' he said.

In 2021, my UPenn classmate Anjali Sud posted a photo of herself holding her two-year-old son just before stepping out for the listing of her company, Vimeo, on the NASDAQ exchange, winning hearts on social media. The picture reminded many of us how work and life are beautifully intertwined, and, in an interview to Moneycontrol a while later, she said, 'I don't strive for work–life balance any more. I don't know if that is realistic. I strive for integration.'

Speaking of being realistic, it's best to recognize that no matter what you do, on some days, you won't have it together and things will fall apart. In October 2019, there was a two-week phase during which I travelled to 12 cities, doing event after event as a part of our distributor programme, Konnect. Early morning flights, days with seven or eight speaking events, nights in hotel rooms checking emails with only room service for company – this was my life, and it was exhausting. There was a big Diwali celebration at home at the end of these two weeks in Delhi, but I was so sick of air travel by then that I told my parents that this time I wouldn't

be with them. The last event was on a Friday in
Bengaluru, speaking for the Karnataka Association
of Mutual Fund Advisors, where I had to give a
motivational speech to 600 financial advisors. I
had prepared a special talk, inspired by Whitney
Houston's 1998 Olympic theme song 'One Moment
in Time'. I landed in Bengaluru, coming in from
from Hyderabad that morning, and at 1 p.m. got a
call from a work colleague in Mumbai. We ended
up having a huge argument, and I started tearing up
in the car, while my colleague, who headed sales for
south India, looked on, confused and concerned.
I told him to cancel all my meetings – something
I never do – and went back to the hotel. I was
angry and frustrated. I was tired of flying around
the country; I was upset with people in my office;
I was angry that my career demanded so much
from me; I was frustrated that I couldn't be with
my parents for our annual Diwali celebrations.
Nothing seemed worth it. I called Nalin and told
him that I had decided not to speak at the event
that evening. 'How will I motivate anyone in this
state?' I asked him. After hearing me out, he said,
'People are waiting for you. Don't cancel. The show
must go on, and you are the showstopper. Take a
shower, wear a nice sari and go kill it.'

So that's what I did. I gave my best on that stage, and funnily enough by the end of the evening the colleague I'd had an argument with called me again, and we sorted out our issues. The next morning, on the flight back to Mumbai, I thought, 'What the heck. Life is short, and I should go to Delhi. What's one more flight if it makes my family happy?' I booked my ticket as soon as I landed at Mumbai airport, went home to throw on another good sari, and flew to Delhi that evening. The look on my parents' face when I surprised them was priceless. In 24 hours, I went from feeling like everything was falling apart at both work and home to feeling good again. That night, while playing teen patti, for the one and only time thus far in my life, I got a Queen trail and won a decent amount of money. After a few burnt pastries, life gave me the perfect cake with icing and a cherry on top!

Among the many different categories of mutual funds, my absolute favourite is the balanced advantage fund (BAF). It's a simple one that puts some money in stocks (risky assets) and some money in bonds (safe assets), and moves between them, depending on how markets are performing. BAFs are dynamic. Sometimes they comprise 80 stocks and 20 bonds, and sometimes it is the opposite.

They do what works at a certain point in time – in the long term, they end up being around 50–50, and they create meaningful wealth without too much heartache. To me, they are also the perfect metaphor for life: Focus on work when the time calls for it and on your personal life when it needs you, knowing that the balance will work itself out. Most importantly, remember that while even the best of funds lose money on bad days and the best of us have serious dips on days that are just not ours, the graph of funds, as of life itself, finally does move up in the long term.

HAPPINESS: BE THE CPO OF YOUR OWN LIFE

'Happiness is not something ready-made.'

– Dalai Lama

IF YOU WANT TO BE COMPETITIVE, THERE'S NO SPACE like personal finance to put your ambitions to work. You can take your personal portfolio and benchmark it to countless different things – not just the standard stock market benchmarks that most people know of, but also what your neighbour earned, what the best performing stock in a random country that year delivered, or the returns earned by the richest man in the world. You can be perfectly happy with how your portfolio is doing and yet find a way to feel terrible about it.

In late 2021, I was having a conversation with a journalist on the merits of my favourite mutual fund category, the BAF, which I have written about in a previous section, when he asked me, 'At the end of the day, why should one invest in a conservative fund like BAF? Yes, it does well for most people. Meaningful returns, no huge losses. But no one is ever going to be Warren Buffet by investing in a BAF.'

I told him, 'But what if someone doesn't want to be Warren Buffet? What if my purpose is not to be the richest person of all time, but live a life in which I don't feel stressed about my money, where I enjoy it to make life better and where I don't think about my finances all day?'

'You have a point,' he conceded. 'Money doesn't have the same purpose for everyone.'

What struck me was the use of the word 'purpose'. Whichever way you look at it, it is key and it is extremely hard to define. I learnt this word from my friend Lara Bezerra, a career healthcare leader across multinationals. One of the things she did in her tenure as CEO at Roche India was to change her designation from CEO to Chief Purpose Officer (CPO).

The simplest way in which I can define purpose is that it is the *why* we do what we do, it is the feeling that comes from knowing that we are doing something meaningful and are enjoying the process of doing it, rather than just operating for an outcome. In a corporate career like mine, it is purpose that makes the long commutes and many video calls worth it, it is the real compensation for leaving behind a family daily and it isn't often measured by a pay cheque. And, as my team at Edelweiss MF has taught me, it is joy and meaning that finally matter at work.

In 2018, our leadership team attended an off-site at Alibaug. There, each of us had to describe the workplace we wanted for ourselves. While there were many answers about culture and collaboration and trust, one of our colleagues said, 'When I think of going to work, I should love it. I should have fun.' He used the Hindi word for 'fun', '*mazaa*', which may be a little awkward in a corporate context, but everyone caught on to the line. Over the next two days, this idea kept popping up again and again, and it hasn't left the team dictionary since. Three years later, in early 2021, after a difficult product launch, another colleague told me, 'This phase of work, what we are doing, regardless of the numbers... It is something! I feel *mazaa aa raha hai*. I am having fun. I want to work; I want to do more.' Each time we feel our best as a team, we end up repeating these lines. And we feel our best not always when numbers peak but when our purpose does.

A young analyst I worked with once wrote on LinkedIn that if you ask most young people how their work is going, they will say, '*Chal raha hai, par mazaa nahi aa raha hai.*' Things are getting on (maybe even trudging along) as usual, but it isn't any fun. This happens, he explained, because we don't know what it is we want, and by default we end up defining success in the way the world defines it – a regular pay cheque, the stability of working for a big brand, a good designation and a nice home. We lack a sense of the *why*. Why am I doing what I am doing?

One of the things my short consulting career taught me is that, for purpose to be an outcome, my choices need to be conscious and deliberate, and that frameworks and guidelines can help us make better decisions.

The unspoken truth about financial services is that a lot of people enter the field not because they love finance but to make a lot of money. In itself, there is nothing wrong with seeking money, but it has to be a considered choice. You should want to be rich because your pay cheque actually makes you happy, not because the world says it should. Of course, for a certain set of people, happiness may indeed be linked to their pay cheque. My father-in-law lost his father at the age of 13, and he grew up amidst five sisters and with limited financial means. When he started working, providing for the family was his driving purpose – and it was a good one. My father was also born into a household of limited means, and for him being able to buy his mother a gold bangle or have her travel around the world is what gave him a real sense of joy. For both of them, earning created a sense of purpose. But for those born with more, a stable job with a good salary may not be enough. Particularly today, studies show that for youth in India a sense of purpose trumps all else – so much so that they are willing to sacrifice a higher pay cheque for it.

If you wish to understand your purpose, ask yourself what genuinely brings you joy and take decisions that bring you closer to it. An internal mandate can come in handy here, something I learnt from the funds business. If there is a law of financial gravity, it is that no fund can do well on every single metric. Finance is a trade-off between risks and returns; no fund is going to deliver outsized returns to you with sustained stability. If you want high returns in a fund with smaller companies (a small cap fund), you should be prepared for deep crashes when the markets perform badly. If you want the consistency of a balanced advantage fund with both bonds and equities, you should be willing to compromise on returns in comparison to a small cap fund. You cannot have everything, so it's better to be clear about the few things that do matter. This is why mandates are created for funds – documents that define what a fund will be and will not be. A mandate document outlines the measure of good performance and bad performance by a fund; it defines the benchmarks, what the fund will do and what it will not. Asset managers spend a lot of time thinking about and creating this document, and once it is created we share it with our investors. After that, a fund manager's job is to manage the fund 'true to mandate'.

Documented or not, all of us need an internal mandate that defines what matters to us and what doesn't. Do we seek money, impact, growth, or a job that gives us time to pursue other passions? Do the ethics of an organization matter, or does scale matter, or do the kind of people we work with matter? The beauty of the personal mandate is that there is no right and wrong answer, because all of them are deeply particular to us. When they are clear, mandates help create purpose.

Whenever I have thought about my purpose, what has helped is to think about life in its extremes and ask myself two questions. The first is: What are the times at work that have made me deeply unhappy, so miserable that I haven't found the basic motivation to perform? For instance, I had a manager at AQR who wanted to be involved in everything I did, right down to the formatting of my spreadsheets. He was a very talented professional but gave his team no freedom to operate because he was very clear about what *he* wanted to showcase to the senior partners. In the nine months that I worked with him, I spent nearly half an hour at work every day talking about my misery to a colleague – something I have never done before or after that. In that time I performed the worst I ever have, and I know today that working with people who give me freedom is essential for me.

The second question I ask myself is: Which are the moments in my career that have inspired me? On 4 December 2019, after 11 months of hard work, we received approval from the Union Cabinet of India for Bharat Bond. At 11 a.m. that morning, we finally got the call we had all been waiting for. The entire office erupted in celebration. A little while later, we heard that at 12.30 p.m. there would be a press conference about some bills that had been passed. We assumed this would be related to the Citizen Amendment Act, which had also been passed the same day. The television screens scattered across our office were playing CNBC, and at 12.30 we saw the honourable finance minister of the country take the dais to unveil the Bharat Bond in a 20-minute press conference. As the employees saw the product they had put their hearts, souls and nights into, month after month, being unveiled in front of the entire country, the joy and pride I saw on each face that day is unforgettable. It reminded me why I love the financial services sector in India – because it provides me with an opportunity to make an impact and make it at scale.

I've been fortunate to have experienced many such moments through my career thus far. NJ India is the country's largest mutual fund distributor, and each year they have an event called 'NJ PBC' for their channel partners. The first NJ PBC I attended was in 2017, at Goa University, because it was one of the few places in the state that had an auditorium that could hold 25,000 people. When the joint managing director of the NJ Group spoke about how their mission was not just to sell SIPs but to usher in a financial revolution, and all 25,000 people in the audience chanted these lines along with him, it felt magical. I had just joined the industry, but that moment helped me understand that this was exactly where I wanted to be.

My professional choices are now governed by the things that give a sense of meaning to my life – the ability to make impact at scale and working in organizations that will give me the freedom to do so. Of course, I want to be paid fairly for what I do, but money is a bit lower on my list compared to these two factors. Having this clarity has made evaluating career choices a lot easier for me. Once again, these choices are mine and are unique to me.

Modern investment theory propounds the notion of an efficient frontier – a line that shows trade-offs and outcomes that offer the best return for a given level of risk. As in finance, when you know your mandate, you can optimize for it, and there is no one right optimization but a whole frontier of them. I have an incredibly focused cousin who decided when she was very young that she wanted to be a doctor and got into medical school in Canada quite early. When she wrapped up school, everyone assumed she would pursue one of the so-called 'intense' specializations – neurosurgery or cardiac surgery. But she chose family medicine, because she was very clear that she wanted a career that gave her time to pursue her other passions and also allowed her to work with children, something she loved to do. She had a clear mandate, she knew it entailed trade-offs (including not making the kind of money a surgeon may), and now she is very happy with the choices she made. On life's frontier, she has found her own optimization.

I am often asked by young people how they should make career choices – whether to take a gap year because they want a break, or pursue a job they don't love but that pays well, or move to a different role so they can make the kind of money their classmates are making. There is no right answer to these questions, but each choice has consequences. It's important to have a framework to make these choices, know why you are making them and then pursue them without regret. If money doesn't matter and you like what you are doing, don't change your job because the world tells you that you are underpaid. But if money is a part of your internal mandate, by all means do not suffer through an underpaying job. Make the change.

Frameworks can also protect you from distractions, because for some people it is tempting to do absolutely everything and saying no is very difficult. The mutual fund business has countless categories of products that an asset management company can launch. At this point there are some 40 categories and that list is growing. Each new fund launched means more money, more profitability and one more option for your sales team. But what we often forget is that each new fund needs a skilled team to manage it, there is always an ongoing effort to review it and there are costs to maintain. The market also indirectly pushes you to do more, because a competitor is doing so or because of the pressure of league tables. At Edelweiss MF we have often debated this, but over the years we have defined a framework for when we will launch a fund and what we will not launch because we don't have the capability to maintain it. We now say no a lot more than we say yes – our framework has given us the confidence to do so. When we see competitors raising a lot of money thanks to a new idea, we may at times feel a little jealous. But then we ask ourselves if it is a part of our framework. If the answer is no, we go back to building the business we want to.

Ironically, while many investors (sometimes led by the media) benchmark themselves to Warren Buffet, Buffet himself has lived his life on internal benchmarks, not external ones. In his biography,

> **YOU ARE THE DRIVER OF THE CAR AND THE CHIEF PURPOSE OFFICER, THE COMPASS, THAT DETERMINES THE TRAJECTORY OF YOUR LIFE.**

The Snowball, he asks, 'Would you rather be the world's greatest lover, but have everyone think you're the world's worst lover? Or would you rather be the world's worst lover, but have everyone think you're the world's greatest lover?'[1]

The message he conveys is very clear. Define your own benchmarks. We live in a Google Maps-driven world in which it is easy to believe that there is only one optimal way to get from point A to B, on one road, at one speed, in a specific time. A fulfilling career doesn't have to work like that. You can choose your destination, the distance you want to travel to get there, whether you wish to take the longer scenic route or the quicker highway; you can skip taking the car, and simply ride a bike or even run the distance if you wish to. Never forget that you have a unique *why* for taking the trip. You are the driver of the car and the Chief Purpose Officer, the compass, that determines the trajectory of your life.

---

[1] Alice Schroeder, *The Snowball: Warren Buffet and the Business of Life*, Bantam: New York, 2009.

CONFIDENCE: CONFRONT THE MIRROR

'Confidence is contagious. So is a lack of it.'

– Vince Lombardi

'WHAT ARE THE CHALLENGES OF BEING A YOUNG woman in the male-dominated world of finance?'

I am asked a version of this question nearly every day – on panels, in interviews and on social media. It seems it *has* to be asked and I *have* to respond. But I hate this question.

It is not that my gender hasn't posed challenges; time and again it has, and not in insignificant ways. Sexism – both conscious and unconscious – still exists, despite the progress we have made. Even if there is no outright bias, there are subtle reminders that make you feel different.

Shortly after I moved back to India to start Forefront, the three of us partners went to meet a stockbroker to learn more about the business. While he shook hands with both Nalin and Anant, when I put out my hand, he stepped back and folded his hands in a namaste. I found it very awkward. As founding partners, all three of us came from investment programmes (with the same degrees from the same school) and had similar work experience, but since I was a woman everyone assumed I was a sales and marketing person and that the men handled the technical finance bits. And, yes, there are people who have unnecessarily commented on how I look and clients who have sent not-so appropriate messages in the late evening.

There have also been times when, because of my insecurities, I have been too scared to speak at meetings on account of being the only woman in the room, or when I have felt out of place because I couldn't fit into the small talk men make over drinks at an evening gathering. All the little and big things that books like *Lean In* speak about in terms of workplace bias have felt real to me, including visiting an office where the ladies' bathroom is broken because women employees and visitors are few and therefore treated as an afterthought.

Yet, despite all of these challenges, I hate the 'what-is-the-challenge-of-being-a-young-woman-in-the-world-of-finance' question, because I recognize that I am not the only person grappling with being an outlier. A lot of us deal with situations where we stand out or feel like we are in the minority – and it may not always be about gender. For some people, for instance, their age makes them a misfit in professions that count years of experience. Enough male friends have told me they have worn glasses, have consciously not maintained their weight and even added a touch of white to their hair to look older because in their workplaces age is associated with wisdom. A colleague who is extremely successful in the banking business once told me that he continues to struggle with how people perceive him speaking in broken English; it pricks at him in every aspect of his life, from his WhatsApp messages to his speeches. When we started dating, Nalin gave me a totally different perspective on growing up in a minority Catholic community in India and spoke about his fear of speaking in broken Hindi – something I would never have been able to comprehend given that I come from the Hindi heartland. Again, as I learnt from social media, one of the most common complexes many young professionals battle is not having graduated from a college that is considered a 'brand'. Each of us knows the feeling of being different and out of place, and how it feels to wage that battle externally and internally.

The question then is: Can we reframe the problem? Can we make our differences, our outlier elements, our strength, our edge over others, and recognize them as opportunities and not problems? Is your young age a liability, or does it make you more adaptable and agile? Yes, you don't speak the Queen's English because you are from a small town, but you have a perspective on India's heartland that many other people do not. Each situation is a two-sided coin.

I want to believe that being a woman in the world of finance is a big asset, because I bring a different style of leadership to the table and a unique perspective in a business where half the ultimate consumer base is female. On a practical note, I also feel if you are the only woman CEO among the 45 others in your industry, chances are that people will know who you are! Since women are still a minority in financial services, the few of us who are here get unique opportunities. I for one have had a chance to interact and interview many incredible women – boxing champion Mary Kom, Arundhati Bhattacharya, the former SBI chairman, and noted lawyer Zia Mody, among others. Last year, one of my male peers told me, 'You actually get a lot of benefits because you are a woman. Many of us men don't get half this attention.' He said this in the most well-meaning way and there is a message in his words. The world is a mirror; it sees you as you see yourself. When you see the positives in your situation,

> **THE WORLD IS A MIRROR; IT SEES YOU AS YOU SEE YOURSELF. WHEN YOU SEE THE POSITIVES IN YOUR SITUATION, THE WORLD REFLECTS THIS POSITIVITY BACK. WHEN YOU SEE ONLY THE NEGATIVE, THE WORLD DRAGS YOU DOWN WITH A SINKING FORCE.**

the world reflects this positivity back. When you see only the negative, the world drags you down with a sinking force.

When I had just joined the mutual fund business, as a part of our PR activities, my media team had set up an interview with a veteran journalist, who asked me how I was going to do anything in the industry given my complete lack of experience with mutual funds. I remember being so nervous I was trembling at the thought of what I would tell him. But, over the years, I have come to believe that a lack of experience has also meant a lack of baggage and a freshness of perspective in how I approach the industry. A few years into the job I started saying this in my interviews because I believe in it wholeheartedly. The journalist in question has become a friend now, and last year he told me that he now agrees with me. In fact, he says the industry should have more 'outsiders'.

There is a poem in Hindi that reads,

Nazar badlo, toh nazaare badal jaatein hai.
Soch badlo, toh sitaare badal jaate hai.
Kashtiyaan badalne ki zaroorat hi nahi hai.
Disha ko badlo, toh kinaare badal jaate hain.

When you change how you see things, what you see changes. Many a time you don't need to change your situation; you just need to change how you approach it.

When I got married, the cover of the invitation used for our wedding ceremony in the Catholic church read, 'Today, I marry my best friend. I love you for your perfections, imperfections and everything in between.'

These lines, which Nalin wrote in 2008, speak something to all of us in a different context. We are all a mosaic – of strengths and weaknesses, perfections and imperfections, successes and failures, of experiences both unprecedented and mundane, inspiring and embarrassing – and while

this mosaic may appear
ordinary to us, it is actually
spectacularly unique. If we
choose to see it in that light
and own it, if we choose to

**WHEN YOU CHANGE
HOW YOU SEE
THINGS, WHAT YOU
SEE CHANGES.**

carry who we are with confidence and celebrate all
that we are, there is no stage we cannot conquer.

In late 2018, I made my maiden trip to Kerala,
to speak at a conference for financial advisors.
Dressed in a white-and-gold Kasavu saree, I made
my way to the event a little early, excited about
weaving personal stories into a talk about financial
independence for women. When I reached the
venue, I was told that I was one of three chief
guests, the other two being Shyam Srinivasan,
the very articulate CEO of Federal Bank, a major
private sector bank headquartered in Kerala,
and the second being Mohanlal, the legendary
Malayalam film actor. I was nervous hearing this
but eventually settled down into the warm and
comforting room. Thirty minutes later, something
in the room changed. Mohanlal walked in. Even as
he remained his humble self, you could literally feel
the love and reverence that people felt for him. I had
seen celebrities before, but I had never experienced
anything like this.

A little while after his arrival, I was told the order in which we would speak – Shyam would speak first, then I would, and finally Mohanlal would take the stage. This meant two things: one, Mohanlal would be sitting through my talk, something you would hardly expect a superstar to do, and two, I would be the one keeping the audience from the highlight of the event – hearing their beloved Mohanlal.

Almost immediately, I started questioning the talk I had prepared. Were my little stories going to be relevant here? Why would people care about what I had to say when there were two stalwarts present? Why did I not know Malayalam? Somehow, Mohanlal sensed my agitation, and leaned over from his seat and asked me what was wrong and whether I needed something. I told him how nervous I was about being there, and how unsure I suddenly felt about being able to connect with the audience. In response he told me just one thing: 'They must have called you here for a reason. Remember that. Speak with confidence.' He reminded me if what I said came from an honest place, people would connect – language, state, gender and profession were irrelevant then. I did what he said; I remembered what I did well and I owned my talk, telling my stories with enough confidence to, at some point, even look at him from the stage. From the smile I got back from him, I knew I had found an audience.

I started this book by sharing some of the mails I get from young people. In all those letters, in all the conversations I have, if there is one common thread, if there is one question that stands out, it is: How do I find self-confidence?

My answer is this…

Self-confidence comes from accepting yourself, rejections and imperfections included; it comes from freeing yourself from comparisons, realizing that you are unique and then playing your own game. When you do, you will play like a champion. In the movie *Dangal*, when the young wrestler Geeta's coach tries to change her natural style of playing, her father (played by Aamir Khan), who knows her the best, objects, pointing out that her natural game is to attack. In trying to get her

> **SELF-CONFIDENCE COMES FROM ACCEPTING YOURSELF, REJECTIONS AND IMPERFECTIONS INCLUDED; IT COMES FROM FREEING YOURSELF FROM COMPARISONS, REALIZING THAT YOU ARE UNIQUE AND THEN PLAYING YOUR OWN GAME. WHEN YOU DO, YOU WILL PLAY LIKE A CHAMPION.**

technique right by conventional standards, he adds, her usual game is getting messed up; it is like telling Virender Sehwag to play like Rahul Dravid. The father finally tells his daughter, 'Attack *karke khel*.' Play in attack mode. My story is the same. I have found self-confidence – which had wandered off somewhere in a battle of comparisons and a quest for perfection – by embracing my uniqueness, and I have learnt that I am at my best when I play my game my own way, in attack mode. It's a liberating feeling, to say the least.

Each of us has an open sky of opportunities; we can fly anywhere we choose to and at the speed we want, because we are all equipped with wings. Those wings may be of different colours, some a little bigger and some slightly smaller than those of the person next to us; they may be a little imperfect. Nonetheless they are there to help us soar. If there is one thing I hope this book leaves you with, it is to look past your challenges – internal, external, whatever they may be – and trust in your wings. If you do, you will realize just how far you can fly – because your potential to soar is truly limitless.

ACKNOWLEDGEMENTS

THIS BOOK IS TRULY A LABOUR OF LOVE, ONE THAT I was unsure would see the light of day. It is therefore incomplete without a big thank you to everyone who made it possible.

First and foremost, my deepest thanks to everyone who wrote to me with such genuine warmth and affection after watching my videos and social media content, and convinced me that I should write a book. You inspired its creation and it belongs to you.

To the team at Hachette India, for seeding the idea two years ago and bringing it to life, and especially to Poulomi Chatterjee, my editor and publisher, who has worked with me tirelessly on every line and chapter, thank you.

I started my enduring love story with writing and with words because of two incredible women, my high school English teachers, Christine Nace and Tina Schwettmann, and I discovered the magic of storytelling because of a very special man, Captain Raghu Raman. Thank you all for the extraordinary belief, the honest feedback and the relentless support you have given me.

My colleague Niranjan Avasthi read every chapter, again and then again, and his feedback on everything, from the cover to the content, has been invaluable. Thank you, Niranjan, for living this journey with me.

This book, at its heart, is a compilation of stories and experiences, and my love and thanks to everyone who has been a part of them. I learnt a lot in my early days, at both McKinsey and AQR, and even more during my stint as one of the co-founders of Forefront. My deepest gratitude is reserved for the people who supported Forefront in its earliest days. A large part of my career – and the most special part till date – has been spent at Edelweiss. Rashesh Shah and Venkat Ramaswamy gave me a wonderful home after the acquisition of Forefront and the very special opportunity to lead Edelweiss MF a few years later – my heartfelt thanks to both. Thanks also to the many bosses I have had over the years, and especially to Nitin

Jain, for their faith and belief. I have been fortunate to lead an incredibly talented team at Edelweiss MF over the last five years. Your passion, energy and friendship make me believe that I have the best job on earth.

There is something about the friends one has grown up with since college, and I have been blessed with a special group, strangely named the Caddoos, who have been a part of my life since I was 18. At 36, exactly 18 years later, I met another very special group, my YPO Forum 7, that taught me about the power of unconditional friendship without any judgements. Thank you.

I have been blessed with the gift of my family. My parents, Yogesh and Arti Gupta, are my biggest inspiration and no words I write will do justice to the impact they have on my life. So many of the lessons in this book and so many of the stories belong to them. Mohini Gupta, my grandmother, was the first working woman of the family. She shaped who my mother and I have become. I am also fortunate to have two wonderful supporters and constant cheerleaders in Luis and Nirmala Moniz, who are model in-laws, and the love of two little brothers, Anubhav Gupta and Sudeep Moniz.

Finally, both this book and my life are incomplete

without my darling husband, Nalin Moniz. Thank you for standing by me on days when I felt on top of the world and on days when I thought the world would end, and for loving me when I am at my very best and very worst. It is because I have you that I can try to live a version of myself that is limitless.

Radhika Gupta is MD & CEO, Edelweiss Mutual Fund. She is one of the youngest CEOs in corporate India and the only female head of a major asset management company. A graduate of the Wharton School at the University of Pennsylvania, a hedge fund manager and an entrepreneur, she has been listed by *Fortune* and *Business Today* among India's 'Most Powerful Women in Business' and by *Economic Times* in their list of 'India's Hottest 40 Young Business Leaders'. Her video 'The Girl with a Broken Neck' has inspired lakhs of viewers. Radhika tweets at @ iradhikagupta and is among LinkedIn's Top Voices.